JANE AUSTEN
AND HER PREDECESSORS

JANE AUSTEN

AND HER PREDECESSORS

BY

FRANK W. BRADBROOK

Lecturer in English, University College of
North Wales, Bangor

CAMBRIDGE

AT THE UNIVERSITY PRESS

1966

PUBLISHED BY
THE SYNDICS OF THE CAMBRIDGE UNIVERSITY PRESS

Bentley House, 200 Euston Road, London, N.W. 1
American Branch: 32 East 57th Street, New York, N.Y. 10022
West African Office: P.M.B. 5181, Ibadan, Nigeria

©

CAMBRIDGE UNIVERSITY PRESS
1966

0521043042

Printed in Great Britain at the University Printing House, Cambridge
(Brooke Crutchley, University Printer)

LIBRARY OF CONGRESS CATALOGUE
CARD NUMBER: 66-10245

CONTENTS

PREFACE

This study of Jane Austen's relationship to her predecessors is the necessary preliminary, I think, to a detailed critical discussion of her major novels. It is the result of research first undertaken at Cambridge, and it was suggested, as I have made clear at the beginning, by a comment of my former Director of Studies at Downing College, Dr F. R. Leavis. The completion of the dissertation would not have been possible without the generosity of the University College of North Wales, Bangor, in granting me sabbatical leave in Michaelmas Term, 1962. Professor John F. Danby has taken a genuine interest in my work, and I have been greatly stimulated by his criticism of the research at the various stages of its development.

Most of my research has been done at the Cambridge University Library, with the magnificent resources of which I first became acquainted as a student nearly thirty years ago. The unfailing courtesy and kindness of the members of its staff have remained constant over the years. To them, I am extremely grateful. During the later period of my research, I have studied in the Bodleian Library, and received a similar courtesy and co-operation. Since 1947, I have made use of the resources of the library of the University College of North Wales, supplemented by an occasional visit to the National Library of Wales at Aberystwyth, and by the services of the National Central Library, available through the College. Visits to Liverpool and Leeds have resulted in my renewing and gaining acquaintance with the Picton and Brotherton Libraries, from whose staffs I have received every possible assistance. I am greatly indebted to the members of the staffs of these libraries. My feelings of guilt at not having worked at the British Museum are modified by the suspicion that my research would never have been completed, if I had gone there.

I have included, where relevant, brief extracts from my published writings on Jane Austen: *Jane Austen: Emma* (Edward

Arnold Ltd), 'Style and Judgment in Jane Austen's Novels' (*The Cambridge Journal*, vol. IV, no. 9), 'The Letters of Jane Austen' (*The Cambridge Journal*, vol. VII, no. 5), 'Samuel Richardson' (*The Pelican Guide to English Literature*, vol. IV), 'Lord Chesterfield and Jane Austen' (*Notes and Queries*, February 1958), 'Dr Johnson and Jane Austen' (*ibid.* March 1960), and 'Sources of Jane Austen's ideas about Nature in *Mansfield Park*' (*ibid.* June 1961). Despite these inclusions, the main part of this study is new and original. The lengthy appendices form an essential element in the exposition of the thesis.

I should like to express my appreciation of the generosity of my friends Drs Egon and Jindra Kodíček and Dr Hans and Hazel Schenk, who have offered me ideal *pied-à-terre* in Cambridge and Oxford respectively, when I have been working there during the vacations. I should like to thank as well the many other friends in Cambridge, Oxford, Bangor and elsewhere, who have also helped to create that civilized atmosphere which both stimulates and rewards one's efforts to read and write.

The patience and forbearance of my wife in listening and typing have been beyond what the most enthusiastic and optimistic researcher could hope for or expect. My sister, Dr M. C. Bradbrook, has occasionally offered general advice. Without the encouragement and warnings of these two kind but stern critics, the project would have been much more difficult to complete.

I am greatly indebted to the scholarly labours of the late Dr R. W. Chapman, and especially to his editions of the novels, minor works and letters of Jane Austen, published by O.U.P., though, in the case of my quotations from the major novels, I have given the number of the chapter as published in modern popular editions. Dr Chapman's appendices and notes have been particularly helpful.

Finally, the efficiency and courtesy of the Cambridge University Press have been exemplary, and to them I am very grateful.

F. W. B.

Bangor, Caernarvonshire
November 1965

PART I

THE GENERAL LITERARY TRADITION

CHAPTER I

PERIODICALS

Dr F. R. Leavis has suggested most clearly what Jane Austen gained from the books that she read:

Jane Austen, in her indebtedness to others, provides an exceptionally illuminating study of the nature of originality, and she exemplifies beautifully the relations of 'the individual talent' to tradition.... She not only makes tradition for those coming after, but her achievement has for us a retroactive effect....Her work, like the work of all great creative writers, gives a meaning to the past.[1]

The question of Jane Austen's relationship to her predecessors has been discussed by Mary Lascelles, Q. D. Leavis and Dr R. W. Chapman. Yet readers of Jane Austen's novels are constantly adding to the evidence of their traditional character, the subject being of such complexity that it is by no means exhausted. Dr R. W. Chapman provided lists in his editions of the novels and letters of all the books mentioned, but they do not include all the books that Jane Austen is likely to have read. Some sources can only be guessed on indirect evidence, and there are certain allusions that Dr Chapman was not able to trace. Moreover, the catalogues of literary allusions that he included in his editions are dangerous as well as useful, since trivial books are given the same stress as important ones, and there is a possibility that the reader will misunderstand the nature of the relationship of the writer to her sources.

The problem is complicated because the essentially miscellaneous reading of Jane Austen is characterized by a quite simple and direct interest in trivialities, while, on the other hand, she was sometimes tempted to adopt facile, ironical and satirical attitudes towards romanticism and minor writers who amused her. The positive, constructive interest in the values

[1] *The Great Tradition* (London, 1948), p. 5.

which lie behind choices involving questions of manners and morals is what gives the novels a depth beyond any mere 'comedy of manners'. Yet Jane Austen's concern with moral values is usually indirect and rarely obtrusive.

Generally speaking, no doubt, she was more interested in writers of prose than in poetry or poetic drama, and in English prose writers rather than in French, Italian or German. It was in the pages of *The Tatler* and *The Spectator*, according to Dr Johnson, that the first model in English prose style was to be found.

Before the *Tatler* and *Spectator*, if the writers for the theatre are excepted, England had no masters of common life. No writers had yet undertaken to reform either the savageness of neglect or the impertinence of civility, to show when to speak or to be silent, how to refuse or how to comply. We had many books to teach us our more important duties, and to settle opinions in philosophy or politics; but an *arbiter elegantiarum*—a judge of propriety—was yet wanting, who should survey the track of daily conversation, and free it from thorns and prickles, which tease the passer, though they do not wound him.[1]

Yet Jane Austen's only reference to *The Spectator* is far from complimentary. The defence of the art of the novel at the end of chapter v of *Northanger Abbey* has an element of exaggeration suggesting burlesque. But it is partly sincere, and the attack on the rivals of the novelist is genuine enough,

while the abilities of the nine hundredth abridger of the History of England, or of the man who collects and publishes in a volume some dozen lines of Milton, Pope, and Prior, with a paper from the Spectator, and a chapter from Sterne are eulogized by a thousand pens—there seems almost a general wish of decrying the capacity and undervaluing the labour of the novelist, and of slighting the performances which have only genius, wit, and taste to recommend them.

The common cant of the young lady who professes to despise novels is accompanied by a bogus enthusiasm:

Now, had the same young lady been engaged with a volume of the Spectator, instead of such a work, how proudly would she have produced the book, and told its name: though the chances must be

[1] *Lives of the English Poets*, 'The Life of Addison'.

against her being occupied by any part of that voluminous production, of which either the matter or manner would not disgust a young person of taste: the substance of its papers so often consisting in the statement of improbable circumstances, unnatural characters, and topics of conversation, which no longer concern any one living: and their language, too, frequently so coarse as to give no very favourable idea of the age that could endure it.

What was the reason for Jane Austen's bitterness towards the apparently harmless pages of *The Spectator*?

There is an offensive air of patronage in *The Spectator*, especially in the tone adopted towards the women readers, 'the fair sex', to whom *The Tatler* had appealed. It was in their 'honour' that the title *The Tatler* had been invented, and in *The Spectator* Addison writes with characteristic condescension that 'there are none to whom this Paper will be more useful, than to the Female World. I have often thought there has not been sufficient Pains taken in finding out proper Employments and Diversions for the Fair ones. Their Amusements seem contrived for them rather as they are Women, than as they are reasonable Creatures; and are more adapted to the Sex than to the Species.'[1]

Jane Austen, while despising extreme feminism of the Mary Wollstonecraft type, would naturally wonder, a hundred years later, how young women could endure such treatment, and how so-called gentlemen could have the effrontery to adopt it. As Anne Elliot, the heroine of *Persuasion*, remarks, 'Men have had every advantage of us in telling their own story. Education has been theirs in so much higher a degree; the pen has been in their hands. I will not allow books to prove anything.'[2] Addison's attitude is that of the Bertrams towards Fanny Price in Jane Austen's *Mansfield Park*. The creator of Marianne Dashwood, Elizabeth Bennet, and Emma could not tolerate such inequality, with the sense of inferiority on the one hand, and contempt on the other, as Addison accepts and encourages in his conception of personal relationships.

Yet there is some justice in George Saintsbury's comment

[1] *The Spectator*, no. 10.   [2] *Persuasion*, chapter 23.

that Jane Austen's 'humour seems to possess a greater affinity, on the whole, to that of Addison than to any other of the numerous species of this great British genus', and his comparison of their 'demureness, minuteness of touch, avoidance of loud tones and glaring effects. Also there is in both a certain not inhuman or unamiable cruelty...a restrained and well-mannered, an insatiable and ruthless delight in roasting and cutting up a fool.'[1]

It was Jane Austen's aim as well as Addison's 'to enliven Morality with Wit, and to temper Wit with Morality',[2] and, writing a century later, such philosophy of life as she had acquired was brought to bear, like his, on 'Assemblies, at Tea-Tables'.[3] As a woman, she had no entry to clubs, and the era of the coffee-houses was over. In certain ways, ideas about morals and manners, education and civilization, had changed, though some topics were still relevant.[4] Addison, however, had a tendency towards complacency and pomposity, based on a sense of material security which Jane Austen did not share. When he refers his reader, with condescension, to 'that great Modern Discovery, which is at present universally acknowledged by all the Enquirers into Natural Philosophy',[5] he may have inspired Jane Austen to parody and burlesque in the opening sentence of *Pride and Prejudice*: 'It is a truth universally acknowledged', she states at the beginning of her novel, 'that a single man in possession of a good fortune, must be in want of a wife.'

The Spectator's discussion of self-love and benevolence[6] reflects the contemporary interest in this ethical debate, which had been partly provoked by the French moralists. By Jane Austen's time, interests and terminology had changed. Yet her fiction is still largely concerned with discrimination between the different kinds of human selfishness, showing when egoism is justified,

---

[1] *Pride and Prejudice*, with a preface by George Saintsbury (London, 1894), p. xiii.
[2] *The Spectator*, no. 10. [3] *Ibid.*
[4] E.g. on the levity of thought in young women of quality, *The Spectator*, no. 254 (contributed by Steele).
[5] *Ibid.* no. 413. [6] *Ibid.* no. 588 (by Henry Grove).

and under what circumstances it becomes evil. She is also fascinated by the evil and self-deception which apparent benevolence often conceals.

In one of the papers in *The Spectator*,[1] humanity is divided into two parts, the busy and the idle, a distinction which Jane Austen follows, though she is primarily interested in the latter. Her novels assume the existence of a leisured rural class, though one that has a function in the community. The world of Addison and Steele, centred in the coffee-houses of the city, is more concerned with the virtues appropriate to business and commerce, despite the rural background of Sir Roger de Coverley, and the frivolity of Will Honeycomb. For the man of business, idleness is the unforgivable sin: 'The Busie World may be divided into the Virtuous and the Vicious: The Vicious again into the Covetous, the Ambitious, and the Sensual. The Idle Part of Mankind are in a State inferior to any of these.'[2] Sir Andrew Freeport personifies the virtues of the city tradesman in *The Spectator* and may have served as the model for Mr Gardiner in *Pride and Prejudice:* 'a sensible gentlemanlike man...a man who lived by trade, and within view of his own warehouses',[3] but Mr Gardiner is an unusual type of character for Jane Austen to depict. Generally speaking, the intentions of Addison and Steele are more direct and obvious: 'Having thus taken my Resolutions', Addison announces, 'to march on boldly in the Cause of Virtue and good Sense, and to annoy their Adversaries in whatever Degree or Rank of Men they may be found: I shall be deaf for the future to all the Remonstrances that shall be made to me on this Account.'[4] Compared with the writer of a periodical paper, the aim of the novelist is to entertain rather than to instruct, and Jane Austen certainly meant to be amusing as well as moral.

It is interesting to compare Addison's description of a lady's library[5] with later examples, such as those of Lady Sarah

[1] *The Spectator*, no. 624.
[2] *Ibid.* no. 624.
[3] *Pride and Prejudice*, chapter 25.
[4] *The Spectator*, no. 34.
[5] *Ibid.* no. 37.

7

Pennington in *An Unfortunate Mother's Advice to her Absent Daughters* (1761) and Clara Reeve in *The Progress of Romance* (1785),[1] and contrast these examples of feminine virtue or aspiration with the comic lack of intellectual curiosity of Lydia Languish in Sheridan's *The Rivals* (1775). Addison's description of Leonora's library is satirical, suggesting the essential frivolity of the apparently learned lady. 'Upon my looking into the books, I found there were some few which the Lady had bought for her own use, but that most of them had been got together, either because she had heard them praised, or because she had seen the Authors of them.' Leonora's reading 'has lain very much among Romances', and Addison looks upon her 'with the mixture of Admiration and Pity', commenting

amidst these innocent Entertainments which she has formed to her self, how much more Valuable does she appear than those of her Sex who employ themselves in Diversions that are less Reasonable, though more in Fashion? What improvements would a Woman have made, who is so susceptible of Impressions from what she reads, had she been guided to such Books as have a tendency to enlighten the Understanding and rectifie the Passions, as well as to those which are of little more use than to divert the Imagination?[2]

Lady Sarah Pennington suggests in her advice the sort of background that Jane Fairfax had in Jane Austen's *Emma*. She begins by a quotation from Gilbert West, *Education, a poem* (1751),

> I labour to diffuse the important good,
> Till this great truth by all be understood:—
> That all the pious duties which we owe
> Our parents, friends, our country, and our God;
> The seeds of every virtue here below,
> From discipline alone, and early culture, grow.

The last line of Gilbert West's verses seems to have been remembered by Jane Austen when she remarked of Jane Fairfax: 'Living constantly with right-minded and well-informed people, her heart and understanding had received every advantage of discipline and culture.'[3]

[1] See appendix 1, 'Books for Young Ladies'.
[2] *The Spectator*, no. 37.   [3] *Emma*, chapter 20.

The note struck by Lady Pennington is, generally, more serious than Addison's. She recommends Bishop Hoadly, and then advises her daughter to 'study *your own language*, and write grammatically....*French* you ought to be as well acquainted with as with *English*; and *Italian* might, without much difficulty, be added. Acquire a good knowledge of *History*—that of your own country first, then of the other European nations—read them not with the view to amuse, but to improve your mind...Learn...*Geography*'.[1] Perhaps it was in mockery of such solemn injunctions to acquire a knowledge of history that Jane Austen wrote *The History of England from the reign of Henry the 4th to the death of Charles the 1st by a partial, prejudiced, and ignorant Historian*.[2] She added a note, 'There will be very few Dates in this History'.

Arithmetic, music, drawing and natural philosophy are also recommended by Lady Pennington. She considers that very few novels and romances are worth the trouble of reading, but when Goldsmith's *The Vicar of Wakefield* appeared (1766) she made an exception to that in the later editions of her popular advice. She also shows signs of having read Richardson, as when she refers to 'the unhappy victims to the ridiculous opinion' that a reformed libertine makes the best husband. Her advice on the attitude to be taken towards religion is strictly Augustan, and would have appealed to that aspect of Jane Austen's nature which was in sympathy with eighteenth-century Anglicanism:[3] 'Aim at perfection, or you will never reach to an attainable height of virtue. Be religious without hypocrisy, pious without enthusiasm. Endeavour to merit the favour of God, by a sincere and uniform obedience to what you know, or believe to be His will....'[4]

The ridicule of the bad taste, sentimentality, hypocrisy and

---

[1] Lady Pennington, *An Unfortunate Mother's Advice*. See appendix II.

[2] Though it has been considered 'a take-off on Goldsmith's potboiler of the same name' (Marvin Mudrick, *Jane Austen, Irony as Defense and Discovery* (Princeton, 1952), p. 23).

[3] Cf. Dr Johnson's description of the hermit in *Rasselas*, chapter XXI: 'his discourse was cheerful without levity, and pious without enthusiasm.'

[4] See appendix II.

obscenity of the reading habits of fashionable young ladies, contained in Sheridan's *The Rivals* (1775),[1] was reflected by Jane Austen in her satire on the reading of Harriet Smith in *Emma* and Catherine Morland in *Northanger Abbey*. Earlier, George Colman, senior, in his one-act play *Polly Honeycombe* (1760) and Charlotte Lennox in her novel *The Female Quixote* (1752) had satirized the effect of over-indulgence in fiction on the female mind. Yet, despite the sentimentality and degrading taste encouraged by popular fiction, Clara Reeve, who herself wrote a popular Gothic novel *The Old English Baron* (1778), could still recommend in 1785 books for young ladies that included *The Spectator*, *The Rambler*, *The Adventurer*, Richardson's works, Fordyce's *Sermons* (beloved of Mr Collins in *Pride and Prejudice*), *Galateo, or the Art of Politeness* (adapted by Richard Graves in 1774), a standard, conservative conduct book such as *A Father's Legacy* by Dr Gregory, and the works of the reactionary Mrs Chapone.

The fact that Jane Austen is known to have been influenced by Dr Johnson has perhaps resulted in an underestimation of the range and profundity of her indebtedness to him. Mary Lascelles suggests that the gossip of Johnson's letters to Mrs Thrale was more congenial to Jane Austen than 'the anxious censor of his generation's morals',[2] mentions the influence of *The Lives of the Poets* and makes a few general remarks about style. Mrs Q. D. Leavis, in the introduction to her edition of *Sense and Sensibility*, notes 'the mighty structure of the sentences', and says that '*Sense and Sensibility* is, in fact, the most Johnsonian of the Austen novels in style'.

Dr Johnson has various comments on style in his periodical essays.[3] The observations on the epistolary style in *The Rambler* no. 152 are relevant both to Jane Austen's letters[4] and to the novels in general. The glancing reference to axioms in *The*

---

[1] Act I, scene II.   [2] *Jane Austen and Her Art* (Oxford, 1939), p. 44.

[3] The standard work on this subject is W. K. Wimsatt's *The Prose Style of Samuel Johnson* (Oxford, 1941).

[4] See my article, 'The Letters of Jane Austen', in *The Cambridge Journal*, vol. VII, no. 5.

Rambler no. 197 reflects the frequently ironical treatment of proverbs and clichés in eighteenth-century literature, an attitude that Jane Austen partly but not wholly endorses. Dr Johnson's positive ideal, put forward in the final number of *The Rambler*,[1] 'I have laboured to refine our language to grammatical purity, and to clear it from colloquial barbarisms, licentious idioms, and irregular combinations', looks back to earlier problems of purifying the language. By Jane Austen's time, there were different dangers and problems. The discussion of faults of style in *The Idler* no. 70 would, on the other hand, provide her with suggestions helping her to attain those negative virtues in style, that absence of solecisms, which her work manifests.

The double-sided nature of Dr Johnson, his wit and seriousness, can be seen in Jane Austen's novels. Wit, as he defines it in *The Rambler* no. 194, resembles Coleridge's definition of the imagination and is not incompatible with seriousness:

Wit, you know, is the unexpected copulation of ideas, the discovery of some occult relation between images in appearance remote from each other; an effusion of wit, therefore, presupposes an accumulation of knowledge; a memory stored with notions, which the imagination may cull out to compose new assemblages. Whatever may be the native vigour of the mind, she can never form many combinations from few ideas, as many changes can never be rung upon a few bells. Accident may indeed sometimes produce a lucky parallel or a striking contrast; but these gifts of chance are not frequent, and he that has nothing of his own, and yet condemns himself to needless expenses, must live upon loans or theft.[2]

In Jane Austen's novels, the combination of wit and seriousness can sometimes result in an apparent contradiction, as in the contrast between the liveliness of Henry Tilney's talk and the sententiousness of a remark by the author, such as 'his manner might sometimes surprise, but his meaning must always be just'.[3] In *Mansfield Park*, two different attitudes of Jane Austen are represented by the seriousness of Sir Thomas and Edmund

---

[1] No. 208, Saturday, 14 March 1752.   [2] Saturday, 25 January 1752.
[3] *Northanger Abbey*, chapter 14.

Bertram and Fanny Price, on the one hand, and the wit of the Crawfords on the other, though in the Crawfords the wit assumes the lighter, more worldly accent that Dr Johnson shared with Lord Chesterfield. It is in *Mansfield Park*, perhaps, more than in *Sense and Sensibility*, that Jane Austen comes nearest to imitating Dr Johnson directly in the Fanny Burney manner: 'the grandeur of the house astonished, but could not console her'[1] is an example of the type of immature, solemn mannerism occasionally revealed in this novel.

Yet *Mansfield Park* also shows, in its explicit concern with moral issues, the essential strength of Dr Johnson as he exemplifies it in the final paragraphs of *The Rambler*:

> The essays professedly serious, if I have been able to execute my own intentions, will be found exactly conformable to the precepts of Christianity, without any accommodation to the licentiousness and levity of the present age.... I shall never envy the honours which wit and learning obtain in any other cause, if I can be numbered among the writers who have given ardour to virtue and confidence to truth.[2]

Such a remark might almost be a quotation from Richardson, who actually wrote *The Rambler* no. 97. Jane Austen's admiration for Richardson's novels is well known. All three writers could claim, in Johnson's words, that they had 'enlarged the knowledge of human nature, and taught the passions to move at the command of virtue'.[3] In *Mansfield Park* Jane Austen clearly wrote in the moral tradition of these two predecessors, though in *Pride and Prejudice*, too, Wickham and Lydia 'were brought together because their passions were stronger than their virtue'.[4] The words used to describe their fate are conventional and Richardsonian.

It was Dr Johnson's view that 'such is the state of this world, that we find in it absolute misery, but happiness only comparative; we may incur as much pain as we can possibly endure,

---

[1] *Mansfield Park*, chapter 2. [2] *The Rambler*, no. 208.
[3] The words were used to introduce Richardson's *The Rambler* no. 97.
[4] Chapter 50.

though we can never obtain as much happiness as we might possibly enjoy'.[1] The influence of his pessimistic, stoical philosophy on Jane Austen can be seen even in an early novel, such as *Sense and Sensibility*, where the moral that emerges is the necessity of fortitude in a world where mankind is almost universally corrupt. Marianne's small degree of fortitude is easily overcome: 'she was without any power, because she was without any desire of command over herself'.[2] By the end of the novel, however, she has learned to govern her feelings and temper by means of 'religion, by reason, by constant employment'.[3] She has begun to learn that, in the words of Dr Johnson, 'The power, indeed, of every individual is small, and the consequence of his endeavours imperceptible in a general prospect of the world. Providence has given no man ability to do much, that something might be left over for every man to do. The business of life is carried on by a general co-operation.'[4]

The realization of the inevitable limitations of the human lot, for which Jane Austen has herself frequently been praised, is the lesson that Marianne is taught. The philosophical acceptance of human ignorance, especially in the case of young ladies, expressed in *Northanger Abbey*, derives in a similar way from Johnson. Catherine Morland 'was heartily ashamed of her ignorance. A misplaced shame. Where people wish to attach, they should always be ignorant. To come with a well-informed mind, is to come with an inability of administering to the vanity of others, which a sensible person would always wish to avoid. A woman especially, if she have the misfortune of knowing any thing should conceal it as well as she can.'[5] 'Mankind', Dr Johnson remarked, 'are universally corrupt, but corrupt in different degrees; as they are universally ignorant, yet with greater or less irradiations of knowledge.'[6] Knowledge and virtue, in Dr Johnson's view, are only increased and preserved

[1] *The Adventurer*, no. 111, Tuesday, 27 November 1753.
[2] *Sense and Sensibility*, chapter 15.   [3] *Ibid.* chapter 46.
[4] *The Adventurer*, no. 137, Tuesday, 26 February 1757.
[5] *Northanger Abbey*, chapter 14.
[6] *The Adventurer*, no. 137.

with difficulty. The necessity of young ladies' concealing such knowledge as they have was insisted upon by writers of conduct books such as Mrs Chapone's *Letters on the Improvement of the Mind* (1773), which were influenced by the ideas and attitudes of Dr Johnson.

Fortitude and stoical endurance are the virtues which Dr Johnson inculcates, though he did not believe in the possibility of a completely stoical attitude: 'It was the boast of the stoic philosophy, to make man unshaken by calamity, and unelated by success; incorruptible by pleasure, and invulnerable by pain; these are heights of wisdom which none ever attained, and to which few can aspire; but there are lower degrees of constancy necessary to common virtue...'.[1] He remarks in *The Adventurer* that 'to strive with difficulties and to conquer them, is the highest human felicity; the next is to strive and deserve to conquer them'.[2] Jane Austen illustrates Johnson's philosophy and moral attitudes in *Mansfield Park*, in particular, concluding the story with Sir Thomas Bertram's acknowledgement of 'the advantages of early hardship and discipline, and the consciousness of being born to struggle and endure'.[3] Fanny Price learns, in common with the other heroines of Jane Austen, the lesson of humility. The visit to Portsmouth shows her, in Johnson's words, that 'few are placed in a situation so gloomy and distressful as not to see every day beings yet more forlorn and miserable, from whom they may learn to rejoice in their own lot'.[4]

Fanny Price's reflections on memory also appear to be derived from Dr Johnson. 'If any one faculty of our nature may be called *more* wonderful than the rest, I do think it is memory', she observes:

There seems something more speakingly incomprehensible in the powers, the failures, the inequalities of memory, than in any other of our intelligences. The memory is sometimes so retentive, so serviceable, so obedient—at others, so bewildered and so weak—and at

---

[1] *The Idler*, no. 11, Saturday, 24 June 1758.
[2] *The Adventurer*, no. 111.
[3] *Mansfield Park*, chapter 48.
[4] *The Rambler*, no. 186, Saturday, 28 December 1751.

others again, so tyrannic, so beyond controul!—We are to be sure a miracle every way—but our powers of recollecting and of forgetting, do seem peculiarly past finding out.[1]

Edmund has already told us that Fanny has been reading *The Idler*,[2] and Dr Johnson makes some similar observations in one of his papers in this periodical:

It is evident that when the power of retention is weak, all the attempts at eminence of knowledge must be vain. . . . Memory is like other human powers, with which no man can be satisfied who measures them by what he can conceive, or by what he can desire. He whose mind is most capacious, finds it much too narrow for his wishes; he that remembers most, remembers little compared with what he forgets. . . . But memory, however impartially distributed, so often deceives our trust, that almost every man attempts, by some artifice or other, to secure its fidelity. . . . The true art of memory is the art of attention.[3]

It is, perhaps, because Mary Crawford senses that Fanny's comments are derivative that she is untouched and inattentive. On the other hand, the lack of attention to the Johnsonian reflections may be intended as a criticism of Mary's general incapacity for thought. Fanny, seeing that Mary is not interested in her philosophical ideas about memory, passes on rapidly to discuss the plan of Mrs Grant's walk.

There are a number of miscellaneous topics that Johnson discusses, and which have either a particular or a general equivalent in Jane Austen. In *The Rambler* no. 137 Dr Johnson argues that ignorance is both the cause and the effect of wonder:

It is common for those who have never accustomed themselves to the labour of inquiry, nor invigorated their confidence by conquests over difficulty, to sleep in the gloomy quiescence of astonishment, without any effort to animate inquiry, or dispel obscurity. What they cannot immediately conceive, they consider as too high to be reached, or too extensive to be comprehended; they therefore content themselves with the gaze of folly, forbear to attempt what they have no hopes of performing, and resign the pleasure of rational contemplation to more pertinacious study or more active faculties.

[1] *Mansfield Park*, chapter 22.
[2] *Ibid.* chapter 16.   [3] *The Idler*, no. 74, Saturday, 15 September 1759.

Here Dr Johnson speaks on behalf of the intellectual, masculine-dominated and anti-romantic society to which he belonged, and foreshadows the formidable sense of Jane Austen's heroes. In *The Rambler* no. 138 he is concerned with the theme of the contrast between town and country, in which Jane Austen was also interested.[1] 'A Lady's wit' (a man who can make ladies laugh) is described in the same periodical[2] and suggests Frank Churchill. The discussion of the art of conversation and the different kinds of conversationalists[3] includes types that Jane Austen embodies dramatically. In *The Idler* no. 53 there is a satire on 'good company' which has the detached, ironical tone of disenchanted worldly wisdom which one associates with Jane Austen.

In many cases, Johnson writes on topics of general interest and it is impossible to prove any specific influence, only a certain resemblance to Jane Austen. This is true of a paper on prudence[4] which is satirical and anti-Richardsonian, and the essay on Spa conversationalists,[5] a comparatively crude piece of work. The young lady entering society[6] is one of the perennial subjects of fiction from *Evelina* to *Emma*; Sam Softly, 'who formerly was a sportsman, and in his apprenticeship used to frequent Barnet races, keeps a high chaise, with a brace of seasoned geldings',[7] distinctly resembles John Thorpe; the discussion of the follies revealed in a journey in a stage-coach[8] concludes with a general condemnation of the folly of attempting to deceive oneself and others, for, eventually, 'all must be shown to all in their real state', that Jane Austen frequently took as a theme.

The language of the two writers, the terminology that they use, is sometimes so close that one can hardly distinguish one

1 See my article, 'Style and Judgment in Jane Austen's Novels', *The Cambridge Journal*, vol. IV, no. 9.
2 *The Rambler*, no. 142, Tuesday, 23 July 1751.
3 *Ibid.* no. 188, Saturday, 4 January 1752.
4 *The Idler*, no. 57, Saturday, 19 May 1759.
5 *Ibid.* no. 78, Saturday, 13 October 1759.
6 *Ibid.* no. 80, Saturday, 27 October 1759.
7 *Ibid.* no. 93, Saturday, 26 January 1760.
8 *The Adventurer*, no. 84, Saturday, 25 August 1753.

from the other. When Jane Austen defines the qualities that go to make up an ideal character, one can see how close her drama of personal relationships is to the Johnsonian moral essay. Dr Johnson and Jane Austen shared a common culture which allowed them to take certain things for granted as understood by the readers. They shared certain common assumptions and took a similar view of their artistic responsibilities. Both have qualities of austerity and asceticism which seem to be almost puritanical in their intensity, together with a simple enjoyment of life, modified by irony and satirical insight, that is quite un-puritanical. Dr Johnson remarked that 'composition is, for the most part, an effort of slow diligence and steady perseverance'.[1] Something of the mixture of élan and organizing ability needed in a successful military operation is shown in the technique of creation of these two writers.

There are certain subjects which reveal disagreements. Dr Johnson, however fulsome his compliments to some women writers, shared the prevalent satirical attitude of his society towards feminism. He remarks that 'in former times, the pen, like the sword, was considered as consigned by nature to the hands of men; the ladies contented themselves with private virtues and domestic excellence...the revolution of years has now produced a generation of Amazons of the pen'.[2] So far as Jane Austen was concerned, there are various hints that her 'dear Dr Johnson' was the source of a certain amount of satirical amusement as well as admiration. Mary Bennet, who 'piqued herself upon the solidity of her reflections',[3] and makes observations on pride and vanity, frequently strikes a distinctly Johnsonian note.

Yet Jane Austen paid Dr Johnson the supreme compliment of associating his philosophy of stoical endurance and fortitude with the virtues of her naval heroes in *Persuasion*. Admiral Baldwin's lack of attention to his personal appearance results

---

[1] *The Adventurer*, no. 138, Saturday, 2 March 1754.
[2] *Ibid.* no. 115, Tuesday, 11 December 1753.
[3] *Pride and Prejudice*, chapter 5.

in a resemblance to the portrait of Dr Johnson given to us by Boswell and Reynolds: 'The most deplorable looking personage you can imagine, his face the colour of mahogany, rough and rugged to the last degree, all lines and wrinkles, nine grey hairs of a side, and nothing but a dab of powder at top.'[1] Sir Walter Elliot remarked of such men as Admiral Baldwin that 'it is a pity they are not knocked on the head at once'.[2] For Jane Austen, however, such characters embodied similar virtues to those of her favourite writer in prose, of whom she wrote, versifying Boswell, in one of her few poems, *To the Memory of Mrs Lefroy*:

> At Johnson's Death, by Hamilton 'twas said,
> 'Seek we a substitute—Ah! vain the plan,
> No second best remains to Johnson dead—
> None can remind us even of the Man.'[3]

Mrs Lefroy, whom Jane dearly loved, 'was killed by a fall from her horse on Jane's birthday, the 16th of December 1804. Four years later, on that day Jane wrote the lines which are printed in the *Memoir*, "not for their merits as poetry, but to show how deep and lasting was the impression".'[4] The death of Mrs Lefroy was a catastrophe which Jane Austen could only compare with the effect of Dr Johnson's death. One is reminded of the famous words that Southey was to write in his *Life of Nelson* and which Jane Austen was to read: 'The death of Nelson was felt in England as something more than a public calamity; men started at the intelligence, and turned pale, as if they had heard of the loss of a dear friend.'[5] It was in such terms that Jane Austen thought of Mrs Lefroy and Dr Johnson.

The influence of Dr Johnson's other writings on Jane Austen demands separate consideration. No later periodicals seem to have exerted anything like the same influence on her, though she was gratified by the praise of Sir Walter Scott in *The Quarterly Review*. Johnson's periodical essays provided her

---

[1] *Persuasion*, chapter 3.   [2] *Ibid.*
[3] Jane Austen, *Minor Works*, ed. R. W. Chapman (Oxford, 1954), p. 442.
[4] R. W. Chapman, *Jane Austen: Facts and Problems* (Oxford, 1948), p. 29.
[5] Southey, *Life of Nelson* (London, 1886), chapter 9.

with a unique type of reading, lay sermons combining the qualities of the real sermons that she enjoyed reading and the lighter,
more frivolous entertainment provided by the usual kind of
novel. Through her admiration for Dr Johnson's periodical
writings, her art gained a depth which it would otherwise have
lacked, though she never became a mere servile imitator of his
manner and style, as Fanny Burney did.

CHAPTER 2

MORALISTS IN PROSE

The predecessors of *The Tatler* and *The Spectator*, according to Dr Johnson in his *Life of Addison*, were Casa's book of *Manners*, Castiglione's *Courtier*, and La Bruyère's *Manners of the Age*. There were, of course, many others,[1] but few that Jane Austen is likely to have read. When she uses the phrase 'eh! bien tout est dit' to Cassandra in one of her letters,[2] could she assume that her sister knew the opening sentence of La Bruyère's *Les Caractères ou les Mœurs de ce Siècle: Des Ouvrages de l'Esprit*, where the phrase occurs? La Bruyère, like La Rochefoucauld, expresses a disillusionment similar to Jane Austen's: 'Tout est dit, et l'on vient trop tard depuis plus de sept mille ans qu'il y a des hommes, et qui pensent. Sur ce qui concerne les mœurs, le plus beau et meilleur est enlevé; l'on ne fait que glaner après les anciens et les habiles d'entre les modernes.' If Jane Austen knew *Les Caractères ou les Mœurs de ce Siècle*, it is likely that she would also have read La Bruyère's translation from the Greek of the *Characters* of Theophrastus. There are parallels in the novels to most of the Theophrastian themes, as rendered by La Bruyère:[3] there does not appear to be any direct evidence that Jane Austen had read the English writers modelling themselves on Theophrastus: Joseph Hall, Overbury, or John Earle. Their

---

[1] See Ruth Kelso, *The Doctrine of the English Gentleman in the Sixteenth Century*, University of Illinois Studies in Language and Literature, vol. xiv; and John E. Mason, *Gentlefolk in the Making* (Oxford, 1935).

[2] *Jane Austen's Letters*, ed. R. W. Chapman, 2nd edition (Oxford, 1952), p. 362.

[3] De la Dissimulation, De la Flatterie, De l'Impertinent ou du Diseur de Rien, De la Rusticité, Du Complaisant, De l'Image d'un Coquin, Du grand Parleur, Du Débit des Nouvelles, De l'Effronterie causée par l'Avarice, De l'Épargne sordide, De l'Impudent ou de celui qui ne rougit de rien, Du Contre-temps, De l'Air empressé, De la Stupidité, De la Brutalité, De la Superstition, De l'Esprit chagrin, De la Défiance, D'un vilain Homme, D'un Homme incommode, De la sotte Vanité, De l'Avarice, De l'Ostentation, De l'Orgueil, De la Peur ou du Défaut de Courage, De la Médisance.

work preceded that of La Bruyère, and early seventeenth-century English prose would be archaic for Jane Austen in a way that French prose of the second half of the century was not.

She was by no means completely out of sympathy with the aristocratic ethos of Lord Halifax's *Advice to a Daughter*, published in 1688, the year in which La Bruyère's *Les Caractères* appeared. Lord Halifax's conduct book 'ran through some twenty-five editions, and held the field for almost a century, to be superseded at last by Dr Gregory's *Father's Legacy* and Mrs Chapone's *Letters on the Improvement of the Mind*'.[1] Many of the sentiments expressed in Lord Halifax's *Advice to a Daughter* reflect Jane Austen's views on manners and morals. Halifax attempts to reconcile wit and virtue. His observations on friendship[2] and pride[3] particularly remind one of Jane Austen's views on these subjects. The section of the advice entitled 'Husband' begins in a characteristically ironic manner: 'That which challengeth the next place in your Thoughts, is how to live with a *Husband*.' Halifax accepts the convention that there is inequality between the sexes, but politely and urbanely shows that there are compensations: 'The first part of our Life is a good deal subjected to you in the *Nursery*, where you Reign without Competition, and by that means have the advantage of giving the first *Impressions*.' *First Impressions* was the title that Jane Austen gave to the novel that eventually became *Pride and Prejudice*, and was meant to be a warning against rash and false judgements of character, but she may also have had in mind this passage of Lord Halifax's *Advice* where he informs his daughter that 'you have stronger influences, which, well manag'd, have more force in your behalf, than all our *Privileges* and *Jurisdictions* can pretend to have against' you. You have more strength in your *Looks*, than we have in our *Laws*, and

[1] *The Complete Works of George Savile, First Marquess of Halifax*, ed. Walter Raleigh (Oxford, 1912), Introduction, p. xx.
[2] 'Do not lay out your *Friendship* too *lavishly* at first, since it will, like other things, be so much the sooner spent; neither let it be of too sudden a growth....'
[3] 'It is an ambiguous word; one kind of it is as much a *Vertue*, as the other is a Vice....'

more power by your *Tears*, than we have by our *Arguments*.' It is a sentiment that might well have been expressed by Darcy himself. Occasionally, Halifax's comments have an epigrammatic force which reminds one of La Rochefoucauld and foreshadows Dr Johnson: 'A *Blockhead* in his *Rage* will return a *dull Jest* that will lie heavy, though there is not a *Grain of Wit* in it.' The sections on religion (the comments are sincere, but antipuritanical), house, family and children, behaviour and conversation, censure, vanity and affectation, diversions, as well as the ones mentioned, all contain passages relevant to Jane Austen's treatment of these themes. The *Advice to a Daughter*, whether read by Jane Austen or not, has a similar kind of attractiveness to the wit and grace of her attitudes to her heroines. Lord Halifax's grandson, Lord Chesterfield, was later to produce in his *Letters to his Son* a conduct book with which the novelist was certainly acquainted.

Between the publication of *The Spectator* and *The Rambler* there are two writers of serious moral reflections that Jane Austen may have read. They are Bishop Butler whose *Sermons* appeared in 1726 and William Law whose *A Serious Call to a Devout and Holy Life* was published in 1728. The problems of human nature with which Bishop Butler deals are self-love and benevolence, conscience, and the individual and society, prudence, the government of the tongue, compassion, self-deceit, resentment, forgiveness of injuries, love of one's neighbour, together with the general sense of human ignorance. These are some of the main themes of Jane Austen's novels. Law's observation quoted by Dr Johnson, that 'Every man knows something worse of himself than he is sure of in others',[1] agrees with Jane Austen's plea for 'candour' in judging one's neighbours. William Law approaches the method of the novelist in the various characters that he introduces, representing virtues and vices. In chapter 7, the character of Flavia shows 'how the imprudent use of an estate corrupts all the tempers of the mind, and fills the heart with poor and ridiculous passions,

---

[1] Boswell, *Life of Johnson*, The Globe Edition, p. 638.

through the whole course of life'. Her opposite is represented in the character of Miranda (chapter 8). Other characters introduced are Cognatus, 'a sober, regular clergyman'; Negotius, 'a temperate, honest man' who 'served his time under a master of great trade'; Paternus, who is the product of a good education; Eusebia, the ideal representative of feminine education; Susurrus, who 'had a mighty inclination to hear and discover all the defects and infirmities of all about him'; and Ouranius, 'a holy priest, full of the spirit of the Gospel, watching, labouring, and praying for a poor country village'. Generally speaking, William Law was too serious a moralist to be of direct use to Jane Austen as a novelist, but he had a great influence during the eighteenth century and was praised by Dr Johnson himself.[1]

In Jane Austen's letters, as in her life, seriousness is modified by wit and humour. Thus, she describes a typical Sunday during one of her visits to her nieces and nephews: 'In the evenings we had the Psalms and Lessons, and a sermon at home, to which they were very attentive; but you will not expect to hear that they did not return to conundrums the moment when it was over.'[2] The juvenilia are full of mock morality, parodying the conduct books and the solemn Fanny Burney. Anne Elliot, the heroine of Jane Austen's last completed novel, *Persuasion*, comes to the conclusion that 'like many other great moralists and preachers, she had been eloquent on a point in which her own conduct would ill bear examination'.[3] Only the stupid Mary Bennet and the complacent Mr Collins lapse into second-hand and trite moralizing, their truisms contrasting with the wit of the heroine of *Pride and Prejudice*.

Lady Sarah Pennington's *An Unfortunate Mother's Advice to her Absent Daughters* succeeded Lord Halifax's *Advice to a Daughter*,[4]

---

[1] 'He much commended Law's "Serious Call", which he said was the finest piece of hortatory theology in any language', *ibid.* p. 216.

[2] Quoted by W. and R. A. Austen-Leigh, *Life and Letters of Jane Austen* (London, 1913), p. 218.

[3] *Persuasion*, the conclusion of chapter 11.

[4] See Chapter I, 'Periodicals', pp. 7–9 and appendix II.

and was, in its turn, followed by Mrs Chapone's reactionary *Letters on the Improvement of the Mind* and Dr Gregory's conservative *A Father's Legacy to his Daughters*. The two latter conduct books were too solemn to be of any use to Jane Austen, except for purposes of parody and burlesque, and she made similar satirical references to Dr Fordyce's *Sermons to Young Women*, published in two volumes in 1766, and which 'became popular at once and ran to five editions before 1768, to eleven before 1798, and to fourteen before 1814'.[1] It is worth examining the works of Mrs Chapone, Dr Gregory and Dr Fordyce as examples of naïve and crude morality.

Dr Gregory and Mrs Chapone agreed on the importance of limiting the scope of the intellectual interests of young ladies. The former invokes the consolations of religion as compensation for the life of suffering and subservience which he regards as their inevitable lot. If women must read, let them read the Scriptures, in so far as they can hope to understand them. If they are lucky enough to possess any learning apart from this, Dr Gregory advises his daughters to keep it a profound secret, especially from men 'who generally look with a jealous and malignant eye on a woman of great parts, and a cultivated understanding'.[2]

In conversation, Dr Gregory recommends his daughters to listen rather than to talk, while in their reading they may cultivate any art or science provided that they keep a sense of proportion, and remember that a woman's proper destiny is marriage. Domestic economy is, therefore, the most important knowledge of all, so far as they are concerned. 'There is no impropriety in your reading history',[3] he says, as a concession.

Mrs Chapone also stresses the importance of religion and knowledge of the Scriptures. She then devotes her attention to such matters as the regulation of the heart and affections, the government of the temper, economy, politeness and accomplish-

---

[1] Joyce Hemlow, 'Fanny Burney and the Courtesy Books', *P.M.L.A.* vol. LXV, p. 734.

[2] *A Father's Legacy to his Daughters*, a new edition (London, 1814), pp. 37–8.

[3] *Ibid.* p. 59.

ments. Piety, benevolence, meekness, humility, integrity and purity, combined with efficient domestic management, will ensure happiness. Mrs Chapone also allows 'a competent share of reading provided it is well chosen and properly regulated. Moreover, dancing and the knowledge of the French tongue are now so universal that they cannot be dispensed with in the education of a gentlewoman; and indeed they both are useful as well as ornamental.'[1] Mrs Chapone believes that there are more agreeable books of female literature in France than in any other country, and that they are talked about as much as English books. Even knowledge of Italian is considered a possibility, 'though in your station of life it is by no means necessary'.[2] The dangers of pedantry and presumption must be avoided, Mrs Chapone maintains, or envy will be aroused in one sex and jealousy in the other. Women should be imaginative, but not scholarly. They may read Shakespeare and Milton, translations of Homer and Virgil, 'which everybody reads that reads at all',[3] and know something about classical mythology. Apart from these subjects, the principal things to be studied are history and moral essays.

The view is taken that novels are dangerous, because they 'inflame the passions of youth, whilst the chief purpose of education should be to moderate and restrain them'.[4] Reading such fictitious stories vitiates one's style of writing and speech, and misleads the heart and understanding. 'The expectation of extraordinary adventures—which seldom happen to the sober and prudent part of mankind—and the admiration of extravagant passions and absurd conduct, are some of the usual fruits of this kind of reading; which, when a young woman makes it her chief amusement, generally renders her ridiculous in conversation, and miserably wrong-headed in her pursuits and behaviour.'[5] Mrs Chapone admits that there are exceptions,

---

[1] *Letters on the Improvement of the Mind*, a new edition (London, 1820), p. 154. This was originally published in 1773, the year before Dr Gregory's book, and two years before Jane Austen's birth.

[2] *Ibid.* p. 154.   [3] *Ibid.* p. 161.

[4] *Ibid.* p. 168.   [5] *Ibid.* pp. 168–9.

novels 'in which excellent morality is joined with the most lively pictures of the human mind, and with all that can entertain the imagination and interest the heart'.[1] She is, no doubt, thinking of the novels of Richardson, so popular with middle-class ladies, though she finds it necessary to issue a warning against sentimentality, a tendency for which he, more than any other single writer, was responsible. Geography, chronology, and history are recommended as antidotes to the dangers of novel reading.

Such were the views put forward by two of the most popular authorities on feminine manners, conduct and education, writing at about the time of Jane Austen's birth. The problems that they raised and discussed really involved the whole question of women's place in society. In a similar way, Dr Fordyce published his *Sermons to Young Women* with the intention 'to engage the heart, with a view to mend it'.[2] The fact that Dr Fordyce wrote 'from an unfeigned regard for the Female Sex; from a fervent zeal for the best interests of society',[3] does not make his advice any more palatable to the enlightened lady reader. In this type of sermon, morality is without the wit that it had for Dr Johnson and Jane Austen. Mary Wollstone-craft attacks both the *Sermons to Young Women*, for their affected style and mistaken precepts, 'designed to hunt every spark of nature out of their composition', and the 'stupid novelists, who, knowing little of human nature, work up stale tales, and describe meretricious scenes, all retailed in a sentimental jargon, which equally tend to corrupt the taste, and draw the heart aside from its daily duties'.[4] It was Dr Fordyce's sermons that Mr Collins read aloud at the Bennets, refusing a novel from the circulating library, protesting that he never read them: 'Kitty stared at him, and Lydia exclaimed...Lydia gaped as he opened the volume, and before he had, with very monotonous solemnity, read three pages, she interrupted him.'[5] Jane

---

[1] *Letters on the Improvement of the Mind*, p. 169.
[2] *Sermons to Young Women*, The Preface.   [3] *Ibid.*
[4] *The Rights of Woman* (Everyman's Library Edition), pp. 102 and 203.
[5] *Pride and Prejudice*, chapter 14.

Austen does not intend to ridicule morality, or to support Lydia uncritically. She merely makes the point that fiction is an entertainment and an imaginative exercise not to be confused with the sermon. She herself appears to have been fond of reading sermons. In one of her letters, she remarks: 'I am very fond of Sherlock's Sermons, prefer them to almost any',[1] and in *Mansfield Park* even the frivolous Mary Crawford refers favourably to Blair's sermons.[2]

Jane Austen frequently parodied the more solemn attitudes and ideas of this type of moralist, particularly in the juvenilia. Mary Bennet, who imitates Dr Johnson and Fanny Burney, originates in a character called 'The Female Philosopher'.[3] The excessive respect for parental authority inculcated in the eighteenth-century conduct books is ridiculed in a *Letter from a Young Lady whose feelings being too strong for her Judgment led her into the commission of Errors which her heart disapproved*; the young lady writes, 'I murdered my father at a very early period of my life, I have since murdered my mother, and am now going to murder my sister'. The anti-social activities are extreme and complete in this type of burlesque. The inversion of normal, natural values does not alter the value that Jane Austen herself set on the social virtues. The humour is double-edged, aimed partly at the more absurd aspects of traditional ideas concerning manners and morals, and partly at the foolishness of romantic reactions against these traditions. Thus in *Love and Freindship* the hero and heroine would have blushed at the idea of paying their debts.[4] It was by means of such outrageous exaggeration that the admirer of Dr Johnson opposed the new romanticism, but the values in which she believed were subjected to the same ironical and satirical criticism.

Jane Austen had certain definite ideas about the qualities

---

[1] *Jane Austen's Letters*, 2nd edition, ed. R. W. Chapman, p. 406.
[2] I have some further observations on these points in a note expanding a comparison made by E. E. Phare (see *Notes and Queries*, May and November 1964, and chapter 4, 'Drama and Poetry', p. 75, n. 1 below).
[3] Jane Austen, *Minor Works*, ed. R. W. Chapman, pp. 171–2.
[4] *Ibid*. p. 88.

that belong to a lady, but they were not altogether those of the conventional type of conduct book. She was, perhaps, more conventional in her ideas of the characteristics of a gentleman and it is interesting to see where she agrees and in what respects she differs from the views of Lord Chesterfield, whose *Letters to his Son*, published in 1774, was still influential when she was writing her novels.

The only allusion recognized by Dr R. W. Chapman that suggests that Lord Chesterfield's *Letters to his Son* may have been known to Jane Austen, is contained in a letter that she wrote shortly before her death, where she remarks: 'Ly P— writing to you even from Paris for advice!—It is the Influence of Strength over Weakness indeed.—Galigai de Concini for ever & ever.'[1] Jane Austen's editor notes that the marriage of Concino Concini to a maid of honour to Marie de Médicis called Eléonore Galigai, her trial as a sorceress, and claim merely to have the power of the strong-souled over the weak, was mentioned by Voltaire in his *Essai sur les Mœurs*, chapter 175, and that Jane Austen 'may have owed her knowledge to Lord Chesterfield; see his letter of 30 Apr. (O.S.) 1752'.[2] There appears to be other evidence that she was acquainted with the *Letters to his Son*.

Among the questions that Jane Austen constantly implies in her major novels are the nature of the best kind of company and the circumstances under which one should sacrifice moral standards and social discrimination for the sake of social harmony. The question of the nature of the best society is directly raised in *Persuasion* in the conversation between Anne Elliot and Mr Elliot, after Sir Walter has been flattering the Dowager Viscountess Dalrymple and the Hon. Miss Carteret. Anne, with the typical lack of snobbery which contradicts the conventional view of Jane Austen, says: 'My idea of good company, Mr Elliot, is the company of clever, well-informed people, who have a great deal of conversation; that is what I call good company.'[3]

---

[1] *Jane Austen's Letters*, ed. R. W. Chapman, p. 495.
[2] *Ibid.* Notes, Letter no. 145. [3] *Persuasion*, chapter 15.

Mr Elliot replies that 'Good company requires only birth, education and manners, and with regard to education is not very nice. Birth and good manners are essential; but a little learning is by no means a dangerous thing in good company, on the contrary, it will do very well.'[1] Lord Chesterfield, in a letter to his son, written from Bath, 12 October O.S. 1748, discusses the same problem at length. Good company, he says, 'consists chiefly (but by no means without exception) of people of considerable birth, rank, and character', though he recognizes that 'people of the very first quality can be as silly, as ill-bred, and as worthless, as people of the meanest degree'. Learning is not enough, for men of learning 'cannot have the easy manners and *tournure* of the world, as they do not live in it'. 'Low' company, he remarks ('low in rank, low in parts, low in manners, and low in merit') should be most carefully avoided.

Lord Chesterfield's view is similar to that of Sir Walter Elliot and his nephew. Anne, who obviously has Jane Austen's sympathy and approval, prefers the company of Nurse Rooke and Mrs Smith, and it is significant that we are introduced to Mrs Smith immediately after the dialogue between Anne and Mr Elliot, as if Jane Austen meant deliberately to underline the contrast of the two points of view about the nature of good company; Sir Walter Elliot, speaking in the accents of Lord Chesterfield, comments on the strange behaviour of Anne: 'Upon my word, Miss Anne Elliot, you have the most extraordinary taste! Every thing that revolts other people, low company, paltry rooms, foul air, disgusting associations are inviting to you.'[2] On the other hand, when, in another context, Lord Chesterfield says that 'Low people in good circumstances, fine clothes, and equipages, will insolently show contempt for all those who cannot afford as fine clothes, as good an equipage, and who have not (as their term is) as much money in their pockets',[3] we are reminded that Sir Walter Elliot himself is

---

[1] *Persuasion*, chapter 16.   [2] *Ibid.* chapter 17.
[3] *Letters to his Son*, Bath, 29 October O.S. 1748.

low in this sense, and has something in common with the Eltons in *Emma*.

Persuasion, as a whole, can be seen as a satire on the snobbish aspects of the aristocratic conception of manners and morals embodied in Lord Chesterfield's *Letters to his Son*. The transformation in the character of Darcy also represents a modification of the view of Lord Chesterfield, with the pride that it involves, and an approximation to the stoicism and social humility of Dr Johnson. Jane Austen seems to have approved of a combination of humility and aggressiveness, such as Dr Johnson showed.

Lord Chesterfield observed that 'with those, whether men or women, who properly constitute the *beau monde*, one must not choose deep subjects nor hope to get any knowledge above that of orders, ranks, families, and court anecdotes; which are therefore the proper (and not altogether useless) subjects of that kind of conversation'.[1] He accepts, though he despises, the *beau monde*, and his attitude towards it is the same as that of his view of women's intelligence, expressed in this letter and elsewhere: 'women, especially, are to be talked to as below men and above children'. Jane Austen opposes Lord Chesterfield's antifeminism as well as his snobbery. One is shown how Anne Elliot's ability to translate at sight the 'inverted, transposed, curtailed' lines of an Italian song[2] typifies her general cultivation. Lord Chesterfield had advised his son to translate, sixty years before, 'every day, only three or four lines, from any book, in any language, into the correctest and most elegant English that you can think of; you cannot imagine how it will insensibly form your style, and give you an habitual elegancy'.[3] On the question of style, Lord Chesterfield has a dislike of 'old sayings and proverbs',[4] which Jane Austen does not wholly share. There is a certain snobbery in his ideas about style, too. Yet both writers tended towards epigram, and enjoyed what

[1] *Letters to his Son*, London, 20 September O.S. 1748.
[2] *Persuasion*, chapter 20.
[3] *Letters to his Son*, London, 26 February 1754.
[4] *Ibid.* Spa, 25 July N.S. 1741.

Frank Churchill called 'the art of giving pictures in a few words'.[1]

Lord Chesterfield and Jane Austen sometimes agree in their views. In *Sense and Sensibility*, Robert Ferrars criticizes the private education of his brother, and tells Elinor that he frequently remarks to his mother: 'If you had only sent him to Westminster as well as myself, instead of sending him to Mr Pratt's, all this would have been prevented.'[2] One wonders if Jane Austen recalled Lord Chesterfield's remark that 'Westminster school is, undoubtedly, the seat of illiberal manners and brutal behaviour',[3] for that is what Robert Ferrars personifies.

In both writers, there is a similar appreciation of the delicacies and subtleties of civilized social intercourse. Lord Chesterfield characteristically writes: 'this useful art of insinuation consists merely of various little things. A graceful motion, a significant look, a trifling attention, an obliging word dropped à propos, air, dress, and a thousand other undefinable things, all severally little ones, joined together, make that happy and inestimable composition, *the art of pleasing*.'[4] That is written almost with the novelist's insight into human relationships. On the other hand, when Elizabeth Bennet writes to Mrs Gardiner 'I am happier even than Jane; she only smiles, I laugh',[5] she may be glancing at the solemn, earlier social ideal, according to which a gentleman smiles but never laughs. 'I could heartily wish that you may often be seen to smile, but never heard to laugh while you live. Frequent and loud laughter is the characteristic of folly and ill manners...there is nothing so illiberal, and so ill-bred, as audible laughter.'[6] Again, Lord Chesterfield comments, 'Loud laughter is the mirth of the mob, who are only pleased with silly things; for true wit of good sense never excited a laugh, since the creation of the world. A man of parts and fashion is therefore only seen to smile, but never heard to laugh.'[7]

---

[1] *Emma*, chapter 29.   [2] *Sense and Sensibility*, chapter 36.
[3] *Letters to his Son*, London, 18 January O.S. 1750.
[4] *Ibid.* Christmas Day 1752.   [5] *Pride and Prejudice*, chapter 60.
[6] *Letters to his Son*, Bath, 9 March O.S. 1748.
[7] *Ibid.* Bath, 19 October O.S. 1748.

In such passages, Lord Chesterfield reminds one of Darcy both in his matter and his manner.

Emma is Jane Austen's maturest portrayal of the contrast between Lord Chesterfield's and Dr Johnson's social and ethical points of view. Frank Churchill himself embodies the classical ideal of 'suaviter in modo, fortiter in re', recommended by Lord Chesterfield, together with the French 'douceur' and the cultivation of the 'aimable', of whose necessity Lord Chesterfield was constantly reminding his son. When Mr Knightley finally judges Frank Churchill's character, he says, 'No, Emma, your amiable young man can be amiable only in French, not in English. He may be very "aimable", have very good manners, and be very agreeable; but he can have no English delicacy towards the feelings of other people: nothing really amiable about him.'[1] Lord Chesterfield wished to make his son 'both *respectable et aimable*, the perfection of a human character'.[2] There are further references to the social virtues which the French summed up as 'l'aimable' in his letters.[3] 'The Graces', Lord Chesterfield writes, 'seem to have taken refuge in France.'[4] Frank Churchill is 'sick of England—and would leave it tomorrow, if I could'.[5] Marianne's romanticism and emotionalism are regarded much more leniently than Frank Churchill's French dandyism, and excused by Colonel Brandon with the comment that 'there is something so amiable in the prejudices of a young mind, that one is sorry to see them give way to the reception of more general opinions'.[6] Frank Churchill is vain in a sense that Marianne is not, though Jane Austen would probably agree with Lord Chesterfield that 'vanity, or call it by a gentler name, the desire of admiration and applause, is perhaps the most universal principle of human actions'.[7]

There is a fundamental disagreement between Lord Chester-

[1] *Emma*, chapter 18.
[2] *Letters to his Son*, London, 8 November O.S. 1750.
[3] *Ibid*. 6 July O.S. 1749, 12 November O.S. 1750, 21 January O.S. 1751.
[4] *Ibid*. London, 18 November O.S. 1748.
[5] *Emma*, chapter 42.   [6] *Sense and Sensibility*, chapter 11.
[7] *Letters to his Son*, Bath, 16 November 1752.

field and Jane Austen about the nature of the moral principles that should guide human beings in their social relationships. Lord Chesterfield observes that

> Good manners, to those one does not love, are no more a breach of truth, than 'your humble servant' at the bottom of a challenge is; they are universally agreed upon and understood to be things of course. They are necessary guards of the decency and peace of society; they must only act defensively; and then not with arms poisoned with perfidy. Truth, but not the whole truth, must be the invariable principle of every man who hath either religion, honour, or prudence. Those who violate it may be cunning, but they are not able. Lies and perfidy are the refuge of fools and cowards.[1]

Mr Knightley, on the other hand, is not content with anything less than the whole truth, and, in condemning Frank Churchill, he condemns, by implication, the point of view of Lord Chesterfield:

> Always deceived in fact by his own wishes, and regardless of little besides his own convenience.—Fancying you to have fathomed his secret.—Natural enough!—his own mind full of intrigue, that he should suspect it in others.—Mystery; Finesse—how they pervert the understanding! My Emma, does not every thing serve to prove more and more the beauty of truth and sincerity in our dealings with each other?[2]

The relationship between Jane Fairfax and Frank Churchill is an example of that duplicity that Lord Chesterfield accepted as inevitable in social relationships. Jane Austen does not accept it, and she makes her protest through the mouth of Emma: 'So unlike what a man should be! None of that upright integrity, that strict adherence to truth and principle, that disdain of trick and littleness, which a man should display in every transaction of his life.'[3] There, one feels, speaks Dr Johnson, too.

During the last decade of the eighteenth century the changing conceptions of the nature of the relationship between men and women came to its culmination. The question of women's rôle

---

[1] *Letters to his Son*, London, 30 April O.S. 1752.   [2] *Emma*, chapter 51.
[3] *Ibid.* chapter 46.

in society had been debated throughout the eighteenth century[1] and the new revolutionary ideas and attitudes finally found expression in Mary Wollstonecraft's *The Rights of Woman* (1792). There is no reference in Jane Austen's novels or letters to the author of this vindication of female rights, though she was probably acquainted with the novels of Godwin, *Caleb Williams* (1794) and *St Leon* (1799).[2] In one of her letters, Jane Austen remarks of a male acquaintance in Bath that 'he is as raffish in his appearance as I would wish every Disciple of Godwin to be',[3] which suggests disapproval. The changes that were taking place were not confined to ideas about women's rôle in society. There was a new interest in the duties and responsibilities of men, reflected in the new type of conduct book. The ideas of Mrs Chapone, Dr Gregory and Lord Chesterfield were challenged by the views expressed in the writings of Thomas Gisborne and Jane West.

Jane Austen mentions Gisborne favourably in one of her letters,[4] and it is probably to his work entitled *An Enquiry into the Duties of the Female Sex* (1797) that she is referring. In one of his footnotes in this work Gisborne mentions 'that kind of courage which ought rather to be called insensibility of danger'.[5] This is curiously echoed by Elizabeth Bennet when she is discussing Charlotte Lucas's marriage with her sister: 'You shall not, for the sake of one individual, change the meaning of principle and integrity, nor endeavour to persuade yourself or me, that selfishness is prudence, and insensibility of danger, security for happiness.'[6] Obviously, the implied indirect debate on marriage, which the Jane Austen novel frequently involves, resembles the discussion that occurs in Gisborne's *Enquiry*. But the resemblance is not confined to the subject of marriage. Gisborne has a chapter devoted to female education, during

---

[1] Virginia Woolf gives a brief general outline of the controversy in *A Room of One's Own*. See also A. R. Humphreys, 'The "Rights of Woman" in the Age of Reason', *The Modern Language Review*, vol. XLI (July 1946).

[2] See *Jane Austen's Letters*, ed. R. W. Chapman, Index v, Authors, Books, Plays.

[3] *Ibid*. p. 133.   [4] *Ibid*. p. 169.

[5] *An Enquiry into the Duties of the Female Sex*. second edition, corrected (London, 1797), chapter 3, p. 27.   [6] *Pride and Prejudice*, chapter 24.

which he refers to 'the sordid occupations and degrading profits of trade'.[1] There was a long tradition behind this kind of social criticism which is a frequent theme in English drama. One of the plays considered for performance in *Mansfield Park*, George Colman's (the younger) *The Heir at Law*, opens with a dialogue between a Lady and a Lord who 'have been raised by a strange streak of fortune, from nothing, as a body may say'. Jane Austen, herself, is very much concerned with the problem of the relationship between the 'new-rich' from the town and the traditional rural landowners. In such a character as Mr Gardiner in *Pride and Prejudice*, she shows a more tolerant attitude towards trade, while in Mrs Elton and the Coles in *Emma* she reveals a similar attitude to that of Gisborne, who describes in the thirteenth chapter of his *Enquiry* the duties of matrimonial life with a view to the different situations and circumstances of the individuals concerned, and considers, among others, 'the wife of a manufacturer, or of a person engaged in any branch of trade productive of considerable gain'. Such a person, Gisborne observes,

is likewise subjected by her own situation and that of her husband to moral duties and trials, which require to be briefly noticed. If her husband has raised himself by success in his business to a state of affluence and credit much superior to that which he originally possessed, and in particular if he has thus raised himself from very low beginnings: his wife is not unfrequently puffed up with the pride which he is sometimes found to contract during the period of his elevation: looks down with the contemptuous insolence of prosperity on her former acquaintances and friends: frowns into silence the hopes and requests of poor relations: and would gladly consign to oblivion every circumstance which calls to mind the condition from which she has been exalted. She becomes ambitious to display her newly acquired wealth in the parade of dress, in costly furniture, in luxurious entertainments. Ever apprehensive of being treated by her late equals or superiors with a less degree of respect than she now conceives to be her due, she perpetually finds or supposes that she finds, what she is taking such pains to discover.[2]

[1] *An Enquiry into the Duties of the Female Sex*, chapter 4, p. 88.
[2] *Ibid.* chapter 13, pp. 355-7.

In the ninth chapter of *An Enquiry*, Gisborne considers theatrical entertainments, musical entertainments, Sunday concerts, dancing, gaming and cards together with the general subject of excess in the pursuit of amusements. The Austens had been enthusiastic performers of family charades and enjoyed private theatricals when Jane was young. In *Mansfield Park*, however, amateur theatricals within the family are criticized in terms that resemble those of Thomas Gisborne in *An Enquiry*. He observes that

for some years past the custom of acting plays in private theatres, fitted up by individuals of fortune, has occasionally prevailed. It is a custom liable to this objection among others; that it is almost certain to prove, in its effects, injurious to the female performers. Let it be admitted, that the theatres of this description no longer present the flagrant impropriety of ladies bearing a part in the drama in conjunction with professed players. Let it be admitted, that the drama selected will be in its language and conduct always irreprehensible. Let it even be admitted, that eminent theatrical talents will not gain admission upon such a stage for men of ambiguous, or worse than ambiguous, character. Take the benefit of all these favourable circumstances; yet, what is even then the tendency of such amusements? To encourage vanity; to excite a thirst of applause and admiration on account of attainments which, if they are to be thus exhibited, it would commonly have been far better for the individual not to possess; to destroy diffidence, by the unrestrained familiarity with persons of the other sex, which inevitably results from being joined with them in the drama; to create a general fondness for the perusal of plays, of which so many are improper to be read; and for attending dramatic representations, of which so many are unfit to be witnessed.[1]

Gisborne's remarks on gaming and cards reflect impatience with the trivialities and commonplaces of the social round that Jane Austen, obviously, to some extent shared, though there is an austerity in Gisborne's attitude that reflects the views of traditional puritanism:

To devote the evening to cards where the stakes are high, is manifestly to cherish a passion for gaming: when they are low, it is yet to encourage that passion, though in an inferior degree. The exist-

[1] *An Enquiry into the Duties of the Female Sex*, chapter 9, pp. 173-4.

ence of a stake, however minute, proves that application is made to
the avaricious feelings of the mind; feelings which, ere long, will
commonly look out for a more powerful stimulus....As the recrea-
tion of the old and infirm, at times when the mind is too weak or too
much fatigued to receive pleasure from a cheerful book or cheerful
discourse, cards occasionally have their use. It is possible too, that
they may have their use in providing employment for the motley
groups which are sometimes assembled together at the party of a
lady of fashion. It is expected, no doubt, that a large majority of
the persons collected on such occasions will neither be qualified to
join in rational and entertaining conversation, nor capable of listening with satisfaction to those who thus converse; and preparations
are made accordingly....Cards too are celebrated for their efficacy
in enlivening the dullness of a country visit. When the dinner, and
the dessert, and the tea-table, have exhausted their gratifications;
when the elegance of the drawing room has been admired in detail,
and the prospect from the windows can no longer be discerned; when
the parrot and the lap-dog have been praised till invention can
supply no additional terms of eulogium; when each lady has already
treasured in her mind every item of the dress of every other, but is
obliged to suspend her criticisms until the departure of the object of
them; what resource, what possible occupation, except cards? To
the unfurnished mind, none.[1]

Generally speaking, Jane Austen was more tolerant towards
gaming and card playing. In *Persuasion*, the novel culminates
in a simple party: 'The evening came, the drawing-rooms were
lighted up, the company assembled. It was but a card-party,
it was but a mixture of those who had never met before, and
those who met too often—a common-place business, too
numerous for intimacy, too small for variety; but Anne had
never found an evening shorter.'[2] On the other hand, in *Pride
and Prejudice* Mr Hurst attempts to persuade his sister-in-law to
play cards, but she declines because she has heard that Mr
Darcy does not approve. Whereupon Mr Hurst goes to sleep.[3]
Later in the novel, when Wickham has revealed his true nature,
Mr Gardiner describes how
it has just transpired that he had left gaming debts behind him, to a
very considerable amount. Colonel Forster believed that more than

---

[1] *Ibid.* chapter 9, pp. 193–5.
[2] *Persuasion*, chapter 23.   [3] *Pride and Prejudice*, chapter 11.

a thousand pounds would be necessary to clear his expenses at Brighton. He owed a good deal in the town, but his debts of honour were still more formidable. Mr Gardiner did not attempt to conceal these particulars from the Longbourn family; Jane heard them with horror. 'A gamester!' she cried. 'This is wholly unexpected. I had not an idea of it.'[1]

Jane personifies 'candour', the virtue which consists in seeing the best in other people and if she condemns the gaming of Wickham in such strong terms, it would seem to suggest that at this particular moment, Jane Austen herself took a very similar attitude to that of Gisborne. Jane Austen, in fact, seems to have varied a good deal in her attitudes towards social habits, occasionally being extremely rigid, and at other times showing great liberality and tolerance. Gisborne is a lively writer and the quality of his works sometimes approaches that of a novelist in subtlety and delicacy.

On the all-important question of the amount of learning that ladies should acquire, Gisborne follows a middle way between the reactionary view that they were only fit for accomplishments and fiction, and the advanced revolutionary ideas of the 'new woman' as man's intellectual equal or superior.

It must also be admitted [he says] that the more profound researches of philosophy and learning are not the pursuits most improving to the female mind, and most congenial to its natural occupations. But if we speak of intelligent and well-informed women in general, of women, who, without becoming absorbed in the depths of erudition, and losing all esteem and all relish for social duties, are distinguished by a cultivated understanding, a polished taste, and a memory stored with useful and elegant information; there appears no reason to dread from the possession of these endowments a neglect of the duties of the mistress of a family.[2]

Gisborne stressed the importance of the home in the life of the married woman,[3] and the cult of domesticity looks forward in its almost religious intensity to the Victorian age, though the attitude is traditional and general in the eighteenth-century

---

[1] *Pride and Prejudice*, chapter 48.
[2] *An Enquiry into the Duties of the Female Sex*, chapter 12, pp. 271–2.
[3] *Ibid.* chapter 12, pp. 290–2.

conduct books. He sees London as the great danger to morality and stable personal relationships,[1] but he is also aware of the limitations and frustrations that provincial life entails. He observes that

> among persons of the female sex who reside constantly in the country, and at the same time possess few opportunities of mixing with polished and intelligent society, errors and failings originate, no less than among men, from the want of enlarged sentiments and a greater knowledge of the world.

> In small towns, and in their immediate neighbourhood, the spirit of detraction ever appears with singular vehemence. In the metropolis, and in other large cities, it may perhaps be no less active. There, however, its activity is dispersed amidst the crowd of individuals whom it assails. It has there such an overflowing abundance of delinquents, or supposed delinquents, to pursue, that persons who are not conspicuous in the routine of fashion, nor by any other incidents particularly drawn forth into public notice, have a reasonable chance of escaping very frequent attacks. But here the smallness of the circle renders all who move in it universally known to each other. The objects on which curiosity can exercise her talents are so few, that she never withdraws her eye from any of them long: and she already knows so much respecting each, that she cannot rest until she has learned every thing. Nor is this all. Among the females who are acting their parts on so narrow a stage, clashings, and competitions, and dissensions, will have been frequent; and grudges of ancient date are revived to supply food for present malevolence and scandal.[2]

In Jane Austen's novels, the virtues implied belong to people who live in the country: the majority of the vicious characters, in her case too, come from London and really belong there. The country is the natural home of liberty and quiet, and what is called in *Sense and Sensibility* 'free and luxurious solitude'. The attitude was common in eighteenth-century literature, particularly in Goldsmith and Cowper, two of Jane Austen's favourite writers. She does not accept this convention completely. The interest in the novels lies in the inter-play between the two different ways of living. When Miss Bingley talks of

---

[1] *Ibid.* chapter 12, p. 293; chapter 13, p. 334.
[2] *Ibid.* chapter 13, pp. 340–2.

Elizabeth Bennet's 'country town indifference to decorum', we know what to think of Miss Bingley. And in the same way, Mrs Elton 'thought herself coming with superior knowledge of the world, to enliven and improve a country neighbourhood'. It is a sign of bad taste in Mr Robert Ferrars that he should describe even the detestable Lucy Steele as 'the merest awkward country girl, without style, or elegance, and almost without beauty'.

A character such as Darcy moves in both worlds. He is in a position to point out that 'in a country neighbourhood you move in a very confined and unvarying society'. At the same time, it is made clear that the fashions of London are largely responsible for his faults. Bingley, recognizing that the country and the town have each their advantages, ends, like all sensible people in Jane Austen, by marrying and settling in the country. The satirical attitude towards the Londoner is what lies behind the treatment of Mary Crawford in *Mansfield Park*. She is surprised at the difficulty, in the middle of a very late harvest, in hiring a horse and cart to transport her harp, and it is she who refers to 'the sturdy independence of your country customs'. Edmund Bertram, as is appropriate, points the moral: 'We do not look in great cities for our best morality. It is not there that respectable people of any denomination can do most good; and it certainly is not there, that the influence of the clergy can be most felt.'[1]

In the country 'the parish and neighbourhood are of a size capable of knowing his private character, and observing his general conduct, which in London can rarely be the case'.[2] On Fanny Price's removal to Portsmouth, 'it was sad to her to lose all the pleasures of the spring. She had not known before what pleasures she *had* to lose in passing March and April in a town.'[3] Life in a town means confinement and noise—'bad air, bad smells', substituted for 'liberty, freshness, fragrance, and verdure'. Even sunshine appears a totally different thing—'There was neither health nor gaiety in sunshine in a town'.

---

[1] *Mansfield Park*, chapter 9.   [2] *Ibid.*   [3] *Ibid.* chapter 45.

The contrast is strongly pointed in *Persuasion*, too. Anne Elliot regretted that her father should find 'so much to be vain of in the littleness of a town', and that Elizabeth 'who had been mistress of Kellynch Hall' should find 'extent to be proud of between two walls, perhaps thirty feet asunder'.[1] It is significant that the Crofts, who replace the Elliots at Kellynch Hall, 'brought with them their country habit of being almost always together'.[2]

London has its special amusements and code of manners, as Mrs Dashwood recognizes when she sends Elinor and Marianne there. Sir John Middleton fails to make the proper distinctions, and, despite his wife's disapproval, gives a ball: 'In the country, an unpremeditated dance was very allowable; but in London, where the reputation of elegance was more important and less easily attained, it was risking too much for the gratification of a few girls, to have it known that Lady Middleton had given a small dance of eight or nine couple, with two violins, and a mere side-board collation.'[3]

It takes a Mrs Bennet to believe that London has no greater advantage over the country than the shops and public places. London, the home of liveliness and gallantry, is where one learns one's manners. It is its moral influence that is regretted. So Mary Crawford refers to the true London maxim, that everything is to be got with money, and goes on to suggest that the metropolis is a pretty fair sample of the rest of the nation, to which Edmund Bertram replies: 'Not, I should hope of the proportion of virtue to vice throughout the kingdom.'[4] Similarly, Henry Crawford maintains that he must have a London audience if he ever becomes a clergyman—'I could not preach but to the educated'.[5] While Fanny Price, on the contrary, 'was disposed to think the influence of London very much at war with all respectable attachments. She saw the proof of it in Miss Crawford, as well as in her cousins.'[6]

[1] *Persuasion*, chapter 15. [2] *Ibid.* chapter 18.
[3] *Sense and Sensibility*, chapter 27.
[4] *Mansfield Park*, chapter 9.
[5] *Ibid.* chapter 34. [6] *Ibid.* chapter 45.

A historian of the Clapham Sect has recently described Gisborne as 'Clapham's ethical philosopher', and quoted him on pride: '"the passion which strikes the deepest root in the breast of the Nobleman", and the root of all evil....If anything was the nerve center of aristocracy, it was the sentiment of pride which underlay the never-ending quest for family distinction, family wealth, family continuity.'[1]

When, on the other hand, Gisborne describes the difficulties of the wife of an officer in the naval or in the military service, he seems to foreshadow the state of mind of Anne Elliot in *Persuasion*. 'In time of war', Gisborne remarks, 'she is left to endure the anxieties of a long separation from her husband... the state of tremulous suspense, when the mind is ignorant of the fate of the object which it holds most dear, and knows not but that the next post may confirm the most dreadful of its apprehensions, can be calmed only by those consolations which look beyond the present world.'[2] *Persuasion* concludes with the brief glance at the difficulties and pleasures of being a naval officer's wife: 'Anne was tenderness itself, and she had the full worth of it in Captain Wentworth's affection. His profession was all that could ever make her friends wish that tenderness less; the dread of a future war all that could dim her sunshine. She gloried in being a sailor's wife, but she must pay the tax of quick alarm for belonging to that profession which is, if possible, more distinguished in its domestic virtues than in its national importance.'[3]

Gisborne's *An Enquiry into the Duties of Men in the Higher Ranks and Middle Classes of Society* was not so popular as *An Enquiry into the Duties of the Female Sex*, and has not the same kind of relevance in its themes to the novels of Jane Austen. One of his admirers was Jane West, whose novel, *A Gossip's Story*, may have been one of the sources of Jane Austen's *Sense and Sensibility*.[4] There are

---

[1] David Spring, 'The Clapham Sect', *Victorian Studies*, vol. v, no. 1, p. 46.

[2] *An Enquiry into the Duties of the Female Sex*, chapter 13, p. 352.

[3] *Persuasion*, chapter 24.

[4] See J. M. S. Tompkins, 'Elinor and Marianne: A Note on Jane Austen', *The Review of English Studies*, vol. xvi (1940), pp. 33–43.

two references to Jane West in the letters of Jane Austen,[1] who may have read her two conduct books. The first of these to be published was called *Letters addressed to a Young Man, on his first entrance into life, and adapted to the peculiar circumstances of the present times.* It appeared in 1801, seven years after Gisborne's *An Enquiry into the Duties of Men*, and is addressed to the middle-class reader, though, according to the author, the middle-class seems to have disappeared and the social world to be divided into either 'the world' or 'the canaille'; 'and, nobody who is one degree above indigence choosing to belong to the latter, *every* body is obliged to shelter himself under the broad banners of the world; and, as the same style of appearance, and the same degree of taste are necessary for every body, why not the same standard in morals?'[2] In previous works of this kind these extremes of society have been generally considered, and yet it is the middle-class alone

whose importance, especially in this kingdom, is acknowledged by all political writers, as giving energy to our exertions, and stability to our constitution.... May she not, as a passionate admirer of that industrious simplicity which once distinguished professional and commercial men, the tradesmen, the manufacturers, and the yeomanry of this kingdom, adopt the prevailing rage for the supernatural, by invoking the ghost of obsolete manners, and commanding it to lift its warning voice, to deter the rising generation from plunging into that gulph of fantastic refinement in which they will find their order speedily annihilated?[3]

One letter is devoted to the absurdity of Rousseau's *Eloisa* [*sic*], which confounds the nature of vice and virtue. Generally speaking, however, Jane West's *Letters addressed to a Young Man* are less interesting than her *Letters to a Young Lady*, which was published in 1806, and inscribed to the Queen's Most Excellent Majesty.

Mrs West criticizes false advice given by many recent advisers of women, but she also has a criticism to make of even the valuable moralists who 'have attempted to stem this torrent'.

[1] *Jane Austen's Letters*, ed. R. W. Chapman, pp. 405, 466.
[2] *Letters addressed to a Young Man* (London, 1801), Introduction.   [3] *Ibid.*

43

She repeats the observation that she had made respecting advice to young men:

The extremes of society were chiefly attended to; and if we judged by the style generally used by the instructor of the fair sex, we should think that the whole female world was divided into 'high-lived company' and paupers, that numerous and important body the middle classes of society, whose duties are most complicated and consequently most difficult, being generally overlooked; and yet the change of manners and pursuits among these are so marked, that the most superficial observers must be alarmed at the prospect of what it portends.[1]

Mrs West says that there are exceptions to these critical observations that she has made: 'among which, Dr Gisborne's Tract on the Duties of Women holds a pre-eminent rank.'[2]

Mrs West's letters of advice are on the conventional subjects, including conversation, society and friendship, celibacy, love and marriage, but she writes freshly. The letter on conversation, starting the third and final volume, which also deals with the subjects of the duty of mothers, duty to servants and inferiors, and duties of declining life and old age, is particularly interesting.

Conversation and its general connection with other aspects of manners and morals had been discussed by earlier writers of conduct books, such as Giovanni Della Casa in his *Il Galateo* (adapted by Richard Graves in 1774) and Stefano Guazzo in *La Civile Conversatione*. In England, Lord Halifax had written about conversation and censure in his *Advice to a Daughter*. Steele attacked playing upon words, remarking 'that which we call Punning is therefore greatly affected by men of small intellects'.[3] Swift wrote his *Hints towards an Essay in Conversation* in 1709, and *A Complete Collection of Genteel and Ingenious Conversation* was published in 1738. Mrs Chapone notes that 'the wretched expedient, to which ignorance so often drives our sex, of calling in slander to enlighten the tedious insipidity of conversation would alone be a strong reason for enriching your

---

[1] *Letters to a Young Lady*, 4th edition (London, 1811), prefatory address.
[2] *Ibid.*
[3] *The Spectator*, no. 504, Wednesday, 8 October 1712.

mind with innocent subjects of entertainment, which may render
you a fit companion for persons of sense and knowledge from
whom you may reap the most desirable improvements'.[1] Dr
Gregory says that 'People of sense and discernment will never
mistake silence for dullness. One may take a share in conversation without uttering a syllable. The expression in the countenance shows it, and this never escapes an observing eye.... Wit
is the most dangerous talent you can possess.'[2] Dr Gregory
considers that humour is allowable in a woman, but that she
should be cautious in displaying her good sense, since this will
make it appear that she is assuming a superiority over the rest
of the company. She should also conceal her learning. His
conclusion is that the great art of pleasing in conversation consists in making the company pleased with themselves. 'You will
more readily hear them than talk yourselves into their good
graces.' Hints on conversation were sometimes combined with
advice on 'epistolary correspondence', as in Thomas Gisborne's
An Enquiry into the Duties of the Female Sex.

Mrs West gives a very thorough account of the correct technique of conversation for a young lady: 'Conversation resembles,
in many particulars, a game of chance. The best players
are those who, still keeping in view the established rules,
adapt themselves to accidental variations with skill and adroitness.'[3] Her exposition, despite its length, is worth quoting in
full, since it represents the point of view of an intelligent woman,
typical of her generation.[4] Her description of some of the common faults to be found, particularly 'in the middle ranks of
society', is relevant to a consideration of the variations in
dialogue that occur in Jane Austen's novels.

In fiction, conversation provides the most important means
of determining quality, whether in single characters, or among
groups of people. There is a discussion between Anne and Mr

---

[1] *Letters on the Improvement of the Mind* (London, 1773), Letter 8.
[2] *A Father's Legacy to his Daughters*, A New Edition (London, 1814), Conduct and
Behaviour.
[3] *Letters to a Young Lady*, vol. III, Letter 11.
[4] See appendix III.

Elliot in *Persuasion* concerning this central theme of the novels, and in his belittling of the place of knowledge and information in civilized intercourse, Mr Elliot is weighed in the balance and found wanting:[1] the greater fastidiousness of Anne implies, on the other hand, that however important social distinctions are, rank and breeding (in the narrow sense) are not all-important. She finds more congenial company in Mrs Smith and Nurse Rooke, than in her own family and their friends. 'Education' (that key-word in the novels) includes more than Mr Elliot is prepared to admit, and can exist without qualities that he regards as essential.

The most common test of endurance to which the heroine in Jane Austen's novels has to submit is the accepting of the world as she finds it, the strain involved in living in inferior company. So Emma notes, during a party given by the Coles, typical specimens of the *nouveaux riches*: 'The children came in, and were talked to and admired amid the usual rate of conversation; a few clever things said, a few downright silly, but by much the larger proportion neither the one nor the other—nothing worse than everyday remarks, dull repetitions, old news, and heavy jokes.'[2] Reading the novels is largely a matter of distinguishing between the nuances and gradations of 'the usual rate of conversation' among such people. As Dr R. W. Chapman remarked, 'We feel how far the language of educated conversation has travelled in a century'.[3] We are also inclined to feel that *plus ça change*.

The question of speech is not so simple as might appear. It is partly used as a means by which we can estimate degrees of intelligence, but it does not provide an absolute standard of either intelligence or integrity. Lucy Steele's want of instruction prevents her meeting Elinor on terms of equality, and the parties of the Middletons and the Dashwoods are disposed of with the brief comment that they did not produce one novelty of thought for expression. Yet the subject of conversational powers

---

[1] *Persuasion*, chapter 16.   [2] *Emma*, chapter 26.
[3] *Sense and Sensibility*, Appendix: Miss Austen's English, p. 388.

is itself touched with irony. Mrs Hurst's and Miss Bingley's powers of conversation were considerable: 'They could describe an entertainment with accuracy, relate an anecdote with humour, and laugh at their acquaintance with spirit.'[1]

To introduce intelligent conversation is a sign of good-breeding. The dangers of conversation in encouraging insincerity of thought, and slackness of language, are recognized, too. Mary Crawford, herself a victim of the conversational vice, sees this: '*Never* is a black word. But yes, in the *never* of conversation, which means *not very often*, I do think it.'[2] To which Edmund Bertram gravely replies: 'The *nothing* of conversation has its gradations, I hope, as well as the *never*.' The dangers are underlined by Fanny Price, who derived 'no higher pleasure from Mary Crawford's conversation than occasional amusement, and *that* often at the expense of her judgment, when it was raised by pleasantry on people or subjects which she wished to be respected'.[3]

The ideal may be said to lie neither in Mr Hurst who, when he found Elizabeth Bennet 'prefer a plain dish to a ragout, had nothing to say to her', nor in Mrs Jennings who was an ever-lasting talker with no conversation. (Lady Middleton is more agreeable than her mother only in being more silent.) Glibness and facility are distrusted, particularly in men. Willoughby had 'a propensity of saying too much what he thought on every occasion, without attention to persons or circumstances'.[4] Wickham had a happy readiness of conversation—a readiness at the same time perfectly correct and unassuming—that helped to create a favourable but false first impression. Henry Crawford, Frank Churchill, and Mr Elliot are also great talkers. On the other hand, Mr Darcy never speaks much unless among his intimate acquaintances, though he is indignant at an evening being passed in singing and dancing to the exclusion of all conversation. Mr Knightley professes that he cannot make long speeches. This is, perhaps, merely a sign of his modesty.

---

[1] *Pride and Prejudice*, chapter 11. [2] *Mansfield Park*, chapter 9.
[3] *Ibid.* chapter 22. [4] *Sense and Sensibility*, chapter 10.

At least, it is suggested that he could, if necessary, shout down Miss Bates. What all these characters (Edward Ferrars, Colonel Brandon, Edmund Bertram, Captain Wentworth too) disapprove of in conversation is the fault that Henry Tilney detects in Isabella—'incorrectness of language'.

The importance of conversation in the novels makes them naturally dramatic. Miss C. L. Thomson suggested a long time ago that Jane Austen probably derived her first impulse to authorship from reading plays, which, however poor as literature, were well constructed, full of bright talk and telling situations. Miss M. Lascelles has noted, in the conversation of Mr Bennet and Elizabeth on the pleasure of being jilted, the rhythm of stage comedy. One is surely right in noting in this close relationship between the novelist (particularly the writer of satirical comedy) and the drama, a characteristic which is continuous in English fiction, which both links Jane Austen with her predecessors, and connects her with a modern novelist such as E. M. Forster or Henry James. Some of the plays that Jane Austen read were, no doubt, comparatively crude. For example, in George Colman, the younger's, *The Heir at Law*, a play which is suggested for acting in *Mansfield Park*, only to be warmly rejected, there is a conversation between Lord and Lady Duberly in the first scene. The newly created Lord remarks to his Lady:

Pshaw! there's a fuss indeed! When I was plain Daniel Dowlass, of Gosport, I was reckoned as cute a dab in discourse as any in our town, nobody found fault with me; my thoughts were like a fat ploughman's chubby children. If folks found them fresh and strong enough, no matter how they were cloathed. But people, I take it, fancy a great Lord's thoughts, are like his rickety brats—plaguy weak and damned ordinary; and want a deal of dressing up to make 'em pass.

To which his Lady replies, 'Why, an oath, now and then, may slip in to garnish genteel conversation: but then it should be done with an air to one's equals, and with a kind of careless condescention to menials'. *The Heir at Law* was first performed in 1797, and by comparing this example of the quality of the dialogue with Jane Austen's use of conversation in her novels, one can see the distance between them.

Some of the other topics dealt with by Mrs West in her conduct book are relevant to Jane Austen's fiction. In the letter concerned with the subjects of Celibacy, Love and Marriage she shows something of the skill of a novelist, and we are reminded of Mrs Elton's vulgar phraseology at one particular point:

An artful woman places her own individual advantage in the first point of view; and her chief objection to a riotous debauch is, that its attendant fever may hurry the good man out of the world before he has time to appoint her residuary legatee. The pecuniary embarrassments of the family are of little consequence, provided her pin-money and settlement are secured by a responsible trust. Her *caro sposo*'s reputation may be irreparably injured; no matter, her own stands firm; she has never interfered in his affairs, and no one can charge her with having suffered her sense of his ill conduct to spoil her temper. Every body is right to take care of themselves....[1]

Though Jane Austen's novels are primarily concerned with personal relationships, involving questions of manners and morals, and therefore primarily related to the kind of issues debated in the various conduct books, collections of sermons and works of moral advice and instruction, there was a sense in which she had a radical dissatisfaction with the limitations of the world of human relationships in provincial society, and she tended to view them with varying degrees of satire and irony. Apart from the extension of her own knowledge and experience brought about by visits to London and to her relations elsewhere, together with the changes of residence that took place before and during the writing of the novels, there were means of escaping the cramping limitations of her environments through the study and appreciation of nature, the artistic cult of the picturesque and the development of her interests in poetry and drama. Of these means of escape, perhaps the cultivation of an artistic interest in nature and the picturesque was most useful to her in providing a technique and method embodying principles that could be applied to her own art as a novelist.

[1] *Letters to a Young Lady*, Letter 12.

CHAPTER 3

THE PICTURESQUE

There was a sense in which Jane Austen believed in nature, even if she was not a romantic worshipper of nature in the Wordsworthian manner. The appeal to her of the taste for landscape and picturesque beauty, particularly as this is reflected in the writings of William Gilpin, was noted by her brother Henry in his *Biographical Notice*: 'At a very early age she was enamoured of Gilpin on the Picturesque; and she seldom changed her opinions either on books or men.' As her art matured, her 'sense of place' became, in some respects, more apparent. In *Mansfield Park*, there is a stress, partly ironical, on the theme of nature and its influence. Fanny Price's favourite room has 'three transparencies, made in a rage for transparencies, for the three lower panes of one window, where Tintern Abbey held its station between a cave in Italy, and a moonlight lake in Cumberland'.[1] The combination of Tintern Abbey and 'a moonlight lake in Cumberland' suggests a reference to Wordsworth, but Jane Austen may also have had in mind Gilpin's *Observations on the River Wye, and several parts of South Wales*,[2] and to *Observations, relative chiefly to Picturesque Beauty, made in the year 1772, on several parts of England: particularly the mountains and lakes of Cumberland and Westmorland*. The burlesque *History of England* by Jane Austen contains a reference to Gilpin and the hero of Charlotte Smith's *Emmeline, or the Orphan of the Castle*: 'I would by no means pretend to affirm that he was equal to those first of Men Robert Earl of Essex, Delamere, or Gilpin.'[3] Charlotte Smith was also interested in the Lake District, her novel *Ethelinde, or the Recluse of the Lake*,

---

[1] *Mansfield Park*, chapter 16.

[2] Pp. 48–55 of which, in the fifth edition, 1800, are concerned with Tintern Abbey.

[3] Jane Austen, *Minor Works*, ed. R. W. Chapman, p. 144.

beginning and ending with a description of Grasmere,[1] to which Jane Austen refers in her tale *Catharine*.[2]

Gilpin was a critic of prints before he became known as a connoisseur,[3] and he published in 1768 *An Essay upon Prints: containing remarks upon the principles of picturesque beauty, the different kinds of prints, and the characters of the most noted masters; illustrated by criticism upon particular pieces; to which are added some cautions that may be useful in collecting prints.*[4] In his explanation of terms used in the appreciation of picturesque beauty, one can see how relevant Gilpin was to the aspiring novelist looking for hints on 'the art of the novel'. Gilpin uses such words and phrases as 'composition', 'design', 'a whole', 'expression', 'effect', 'spirit', 'manner', 'picturesque', 'picturesque grace', 'repose or quietness', 'to keep down, take down, or bring down' ('throwing a degree of shade upon a glaring light'), 'a middle tint' ('a medium between a strong light, and strong shade'), 'catching lights' ('strong lights which strike upon some particular parts of an object, the rest of which is shadow'), 'studies', 'freedom' ('the result of quick execution'), 'air' ('the graceful action of the head', 'a graceful attitude'), and 'contrast'. When Jane Austen remarks in *Northanger Abbey* that 'the rules of composition forbid the introduction of a character not connected with my fable', she may have had in mind the sort of rules laid down in Hugh Blair's *Lectures on Rhetoric and Belles Lettres* (1783), but she would almost certainly have also remembered Gilpin's definition, 'Composition; in its *large* sense, means a picture in general: in its *limited* one, the art of grouping figures and combining the parts of a picture'.[5]

Gilpin includes in his third chapter, 'Characters of the most noted Masters', a critical examination of the works of 'our most celebrated countryman, Hogarth.' 'In *composition* we see

---

[1] This is pointed out by Dr R. W. Chapman in Jane Austen, *Minor Works*, 'Notes', p. 460.

[2] Jane Austen, *Minor Works*, p. 199.

[3] See chapter v, *The Life and Work of William Gilpin*, by William D. Templeman (University of Illinois Press, 1939).

[4] See appendix IV below.

[5] William Gilpin, *An Essay upon Prints* (London, 1768), 'Explanation of Terms'.

little in him to admire', though 'no one could tell a story better; or make it, in all its circumstances, more intelligible. His genius, however, it must be owned, was suited only to *low* or *familiar* subjects. It never soared above *common* life.' Hogarth's art was certainly 'low' in a sense that would be uncongenial to the more selective and discriminating artistry of Jane Austen. He was closer to the more crudely realistic fictional worlds of Richardson, Fielding, Smollett and Dickens.[1] Yet 'with instances of picturesque grace his works abound',[2] and his ability to tell a story was, no doubt, noted, if not directly appreciated. Gilpin refers to Hogarth's humour, satire, moral lessons and 'fund of entertainment suited to every taste; a circumstance, which shows them to be just copies of nature. We may consider them too as valuable repositories of the manners, customs, and dresses of the present age.'[3] This kind of critical examination could easily be transferred and applied to the criticism of fiction.

The principles of painting, in so far as they relate to prints, demand, according to Gilpin, a sense of the effect of the work of art as a whole. To achieve this, a just observance of those rules is necessary, which relate to design, disposition, 'keeping', and the distribution of light. By design is meant 'a proper time, proper characters, the most affecting manner of introducing those characters, and proper appendages'. To make a print agreeable in its parts, the artist has also to observe the rules relating to 'drawing, expression, grace, and perspective'.

Gilpin's three essays, on picturesque beauty, on picturesque travel, and on sketching landscape, to which is added a poem on landscape painting (1792), reveal further ways in which the cult of the picturesque provided Jane Austen with ideas which were related to the problems she had to solve as a novelist. 'A truth is a truth', Gilpin remarks, 'whether delivered in the

---

[1] 'Hogarth was one of the sources of life and shaping inspiration from the English past that gave Dickens, as a novelist in the English tradition, such immense advantage over any French contemporary' (F. R. Leavis, 'Dombey and Son', *The Sewanee Review*, vol. LXX, no. 2, p. 197).

[2] William Gilpin, *An Essay upon Prints*, p. 173.   [3] *Ibid.* p. 168.

language of a philosopher or of a peasant, and the intellect receives it as such. But the artist, who deals in lines, surfaces and colours, which are an immediate address to the eye, conceives the *very truth itself* concerned in his *mode* of representing it.'[1] A precise definition of the meaning of the term picturesque beauty is given in *Observations on the Western Parts of England, relative chiefly to Picturesque Beauty*: 'Picturesque beauty is a phrase but a little understood. We precisely mean by it that kind of beauty which *would look well in a picture*. Neither grounds laid out by art, nor improved by agriculture, are of this kind.'[2]

The picturesque distinction between the rough and the smooth surface, where the rough is more important as providing the necessary element of variety in composition, has its equivalent in fiction in the types of contrast that occur between an Edmund Bertram and a Henry Crawford, a Mr Knightley and a Frank Churchill, a Mr Elliot and a Captain Wentworth. Light and shade are provided by the constantly changing combinations of character and action, while the volumes into which the novels were originally divided constitute the foreground, middle ground and distance of Jane Austen's fictionalized pictures.[3]

Gilpin himself observes that

language, like light, is a medium: and the true philosophic stile, like light from a north-window, exhibits objects clearly and distinctly, without soliciting attention to itself. In painting subjects of amusement indeed, language may guild somewhat more and colour with the dies of fancy; but where information is of more importance than entertainment, though you cannot throw too strong a light, you should carefully avoid a *coloured* one. The stile of some writers resembles a bright light placed between the eye and the thing to be

---

[1] *Three Essays on Picturesque Beauty*... (London, 1792), pp. 18–19.
[2] *Observations on Western Parts of England*... (London, 1798), sect. xxxv, p. 328.
[3] It is interesting to see American critics using the terminology of the picturesque without apparently realizing its importance. Prof. Wayne C. Booth writes on 'Point of View and Control of Distance in *Emma*', without mentioning Gilpin. Similarly E. M. Halliday discusses 'Narrative Perspective in *Pride and Prejudice*' (*Nineteenth-Century Fiction*, vols. 16, no. 2 and 15, no. 1).

looked at. The light shows itself; and hides the object: and it must be allowed the execution of some painters is as impertinent as the stile of such writers.[1]

Jane Austen commands 'the true philosophic style' in Gilpin's sense.

The perfect justification of the type of fiction that Jane Austen wrote is put forward by Gilpin in his essay on picturesque travel.

Some artists [he remarks], when they give their imagination play, let it loose among uncommon scenes—such as perhaps never existed: whereas the nearer they approach the simple standard of nature in its most beautiful forms, the more admirable their fictions will appear. It is thus in writing romances. The correct taste cannot bear those unnatural situations in which heroes and heroines are often placed, whereas a story *naturally* and of course affectingly told, either with a pen or a pencil, though known to be a fiction, is considered as a transcript from nature; and takes possession of the heart. The *marvellous* disgusts the sober imagination; which is gratified only with the pure characters of nature.[2]

In the poem on landscape painting, Gilpin stresses the importance of a balance of parts, of simplicity as opposed to too much variety, and the choice of a particular scene or leading subject, to which the parts should be subservient. Twelve years earlier, in 1780, Horace Walpole had published *The History of Modern Taste in Gardening*, and celebrated the new beauties of the English landscape.

How rich, how gay, how picturesque the face of the country! The demolition of walls laying open each improvement, every journey is made through a succession of pictures; and even where taste is wanting in the spot improved, the general view is embellished by variety. If no relapse to barbarism, formality, and seclusion, is made, what landscapes will dignify every quarter of our island, when the daily plantations that are making have attained venerable maturity! A specimen of what our gardens will be, may be seen at Petworth, where the portion of the park nearest the house has been allotted

---

[1] *Three Essays on Picturesque Beauty...*, note, p. 18.
[2] *Ibid.* pp. 52–3.

to the modern style. It is a garden of oaks two hundred years old. If there is a fault in so august a fragment of improved nature, it is, that the size of the trees are out of all proportion to the shrubs and accompanyments. In truth, shrubs should not only be preserved for particular spots and home delight, but are past their beauty in less than twenty years.

Enough has been done to establish such a school of landscape, as cannot be found on the rest of the globe. If we have the seeds of a Claud or a Gaspar amongst us, he must come forth. If wood, water, groves, vallies, glades, can inspire or poet or painter, this is the country, this is the age to produce them. The flocks, the herds, that now are admitted into, now graze on the borders of our cultivated plains, are ready before the painter's eyes, and groupe [*sic*] themselves to animate his picture. One misfortune in truth there is that throws a difficulty on the artist. A principal beauty in our gardens is the lawn and smoothness of turf: in a picture it becomes a dead and uniform spot, incapable of chiaro scuro, and to be broken insipidly by children, dogs, and other unmeaning figures.

Since we have been familiarized to the study of landscape, we hear less of what delighted our sportsmen-ancestors, *a fine open country*. Wiltshire, Dorsetshire, and such ocean-like extents were formerly preferred to the rich blue prospects of Kent, to the Thames-watered views in Berkshire, and to the magnificent scale of nature in Yorkshire. An open country is but a canvas on which a landscape might be designed.[1]

Jane Austen satirized the enthusiasm for the picturesque, but she also took some of its more absurd ideas half seriously, at times. Thus, William Shenstone has a passage on trees in one of his essays, which develops an idea that is sometimes burlesqued and sometimes taken seriously.

All trees have a character analogous to that of men [he says]. Oaks are in all respects the perfect image of the manly character: in former times I should have said, and in present times I think I am authorized to say, the British one. As a brave man is not suddenly either elated by prosperity or depressed by adversity, so the oak displays not its verdure on the sun's first approach; nor drops it, on his first departure. Add to this its majestic appearance, the rough

---

[1] *Horace Walpole, Gardenist.* An edition of Walpole's *The History of Modern Taste in Gardening* with an Estimate of Walpole's Contribution to Landscape Architecture, by Isabel W. U. Chase (Princeton, 1943), pp. 36-7.

grandeur of its bark, and the wide protection of its branches. A large, branching aged oak is perhaps the most venerable of all inanimate objects.[1]

In Jane Austen's early burlesque, *Love and Freindship*, when Laura and Sophia are sheltering 'from the Eastern Zephyr', the former draws attention to 'the noble grandeur of the elms'. Sophia replies, 'Do not wound my sensibility by observing on those elms. They remind me of Augustus. He was like them, tall, majestic—he possessed that noble grandeur which you admire in them'. The sky itself 'cruelly' reminds Sophia of Augustus' blue satin waistcoat striped with white.[2] On the other hand, there is a certain degree of seriousness in Edward Ferrars's criticism of the wild scenery of the terror and horror novels: 'I do not like crooked, twisted, blasted trees. I admire them much more if they are tall, straight and flourishing.'[3] Despite his sense, Edward Ferrars shares some of Sophia's romanticism, as does Jane Austen herself. When Elinor and Marianne returned to Cleveland towards the end of *Sense and Sensibility*, 'the house itself was under the guardianship of the fir, the mountain-ash, and the acacia, and the thick screen of them altogether, interspersed with tall Lombardy poplars, shut out the offices'.[4] When Marianne asks who will remain at Norland to enjoy the trees, she is voicing the sentiments of her creator. Darcy has his beautiful oaks and Spanish chestnuts at Pemberley,[5] no doubt, like him, tall and majestic, while in Fanny Price's reveries there is reflected in slightly exaggerated form Jane Austen's own taste: 'Cut down an avenue! What a pity! Does it not make you think of Cowper? "Ye fallen avenues, once more I mourn your fate unmerited".'[6] These lines from Cowper's *The Task*[7] had also been quoted by Gilpin in his *Observations on the Western Parts of England, relative chiefly to Picturesque Beauty*, as Dr R. W. Chapman noted.[8] There is an

---

[1] William Shenstone, *Essays on Men and Manners* (London, 1802), p. 105.
[2] Jane Austen, *Minor Works*, p. 98.   [3] *Sense and Sensibility*, chapter 18.
[4] *Ibid.* chapter 42.   [5] *Pride and Prejudice*, chapter 45.
[6] *Mansfield Park*, chapter 6.   [7] *The Task*, Book 1, 'The Sofa', ll. 338–9.
[8] See his edition of *Mansfield Park*, 'Notes', p. 542.

element of ironical exaggeration, however, in Jane Austen's use of Cowper, which distinguishes her treatment of nature from his, and that of Gilpin.

The observations that Gilpin made during his various journeys in search of the picturesque provided Jane Austen with a knowledge of the country additional to that which she gained in her own travels. She made use of these sources much more frequently and thoroughly than appears to have been recognized. She also made satirical references to Gilpin, as well as to the cult of the picturesque in general. Gilpin was inclined, at times, to be slightly solemn and pompous, taking himself and the cult of the picturesque with too much seriousness for his ironical reader. Thus, he observes in the preface to *The Observations on the Mountains and Lakes of Cumberland and Westmorland*: 'The author hopes no one will be so severe, as to think a work of this kind (tho' a work only of amusement) inconsistent with the profession of a clergyman.' Again, he comments in the preface, 'The author however hopes, he should not greatly err, if he allowed also the amusements furnished by the three sister-arts, to be all very consistent with the strictest rules of the clerical profession'. Jane Austen appears to have recalled these passages when she wrote the sublime nonsense of Mr Collins in *Pride and Prejudice*: '"If I", said Mr Collins, "were so fortunate as to be able to sing, I should have great pleasure, I am sure, in obliging the company with an air; for I consider music as a very innocent diversion, and perfectly compatible with the profession of a clergyman".'[1] Similarly, Gilpin had expressed concern at the possible lack of seriousness encouraged by an interest in the picturesque: 'The only danger is, lest the *amusement*—the fascinating amusement—should press on improperly, and interfere too much with the *employment*.'[2]

Gilpin makes occasional mistakes of tone and attitude of this kind, but in discussing the aesthetic characteristics of landscape

[1] Chapter 18.
[2] *Observations on the Mountains and Lakes of Cumberland and Westmorland* (London, 1786), Preface, pp. xxii–xxiii.

in his observations, he provided Jane Austen with an example of artistic method from which she could learn. Thus, he remarks,

In a distance the ruling character is *tenderness*; which on a *fore-ground*, gives way to what the painter calls *force*, and *richness*. *Force* arises from a violent opposition of colour, light, and shade: *richness*, consists in a variety of parts, and glowing tints. In some degree, *richness* is found in a distance; but never, united with *force*: for in a *distance*; tho' the *lights* may be strong, and the parts varied; yet the shades and tints will never be faint, and tender.

In the mean time, this opposition on the foreground, violent as it is, must always be subject to the *ruling masses* of light and shade, and colouring, which harmonize the whole.[1]

There are ways in which Jane Austen derives more simply and directly from Gilpin. In the *Observations on the Mountains and Lakes of Cumberland and Westmorland*, there is a general description of the Peak of Derbyshire. This is a part of the country which Jane Austen does not seem to have known or visited, though her brother Henry was in Matlock in 1813.[2] Yet in *Pride and Prejudice*, at the end of the second volume, the action suddenly moves to Derbyshire:

In that county, there was enough to be seen, to occupy the chief of their three weeks: and to Mrs Gardiner it had a peculiarly strong attraction. The town where she had formerly passed some years of her life, and where they were now to spend a few days was probably as great an object of her curiosity, as all the celebrated beauties of Matlock, Chatsworth, Dovedale, or the Peak.[3]

It is in Derbyshire that Pemberley, the country house of Darcy, is situated, and it has some of the finest woods in the country.

When Elizabeth meets Darcy at Pemberley, she says, 'before we left Bakewell, we understood that you were not immediately expected in the country'.[4] Gilpin mentions Bakewell and goes on to describe Haddon Hall, which would seem, therefore, to be a possible model for Pemberley itself. Haddon Hall is a 'magnificent old mansion' standing on a rocky knoll en-

---

[1] *Observations on the Mountains and Lakes of Cumberland and Westmorland*, sect. VIII, vol. I, pp. 103–4.
[2] *Jane Austen's Letters*, ed. R. W. Chapman, p. 326.
[3] *Pride and Prejudice*, chapter 42.   [4] *Ibid.* chapter 43.

compassed with wood, a 'princely structure, scarce yet in a state of ruin'.[1] This account is followed by a description of Chatsworth, 'in a situation naturally bleak; but rendered not unpleasant by its accompaniments of well-grown wood'. Chatsworth, Gilpin says, was the glory of the last age, but its environs had not kept pace with the improvements of the times. Gilpin then travels through Darley-dale, 'a sweet, extensive scene', and approaches Matlock:

...the vale of Matlock; a romantic, and most delightful scene, in which the ideas of sublimity and beauty are blended in a high degree.

It is impossible to view such scenes as these, without feeling the imagination take fire. Little fairy scenes, where the parts, tho' trifling, are happily disposed: such, for instance, as the cascade-scene in the gardens at the Leasowes, please the fancy. But this is scenery of a different kind. Every object here, is sublime, and wonderful. Not only the eye is pleased; but the imagination is filled. We are carried at once into the fields of fiction, and romance. Enthusiastic ideas take possession of us; and we suppose ourselves among the inhabitants of fabled times.—The transition indeed is easy and natural, from romantic scenes to romantic inhabitants.[2]

It is against such a background of romance, sublimity, beauty and delight that the hero and heroine of *Pride and Prejudice* are reconciled.

For Gilpin, the Peak is 'wild' as well as beautiful, great and noble. As a contrast he describes the pleasant road to Ashburn, where 'the ground is varied, and adorned with wood'. Ashburn, which is among the larger villages, 'stands sweetly', and from there he made an excursion to Dove-dale, remarking that it is in scenery, as in life: we are most struck with the peculiarity of an original character, provided there is nothing offensive in it.

Dr R. W. Chapman states that Mansfield Park may be identified with Cottesbrooke, in the county of Northamptonshire, with whose owner, Sir James Langham, Jane Austen's

[1] *Observations on the Mountains and Lakes of Cumberland and Westmorland*, sect. xxviii, 'General description of the Peak of Derbyshire', vol. ii, p. 219.
[2] *Ibid*, pp. 221-3.

brother Henry was acquainted.[1] In Jane Austen's letters there are two inquiries in January and February 1813 to Cassandra and Martha Lloyd about Northamptonshire.[2] She writes to Cassandra, saying that she would be glad if her sister could discover whether Northamptonshire is a country of hedgerows. The writing of *Mansfield Park* was finished soon after June 1813 and, perhaps, Jane Austen wished to confirm that the country-side was in a similar state to Gilpin's description, made in 1772. For in his *Observations on the Mountains and Lakes of Cumberland and Westmorland*, Gilpin has a description of the journey back to London during which he describes Lord Strafford's gardens in Northamptonshire 'extending a considerable way on the left' and which are a great ornament to the county. Then he goes on to observe that Lord Halifax's improvements succeed:

They make little appearance from the road: but the road itself is so beautiful, that it requires no aid. It passes through spacious lanes, adorned on each side by a broad, irregular border of grass; and winds through hedge-rows of full-grown oak, which the several turns of the road form into clumps. You have both a good foreground, and beautiful views into a fine country, through the boles of the trees. The undressed simplicity, and native beauty, of such lanes as these, exceed the walks of the most finished garden.[3]

The approach to London evokes a horror and disgust in Gilpin that is worthy of Cobbett and which would have been read with appreciation and approval by Jane Austen herself, although in *Pride and Prejudice* the Gardiners live in London. Jane Austen usually regarded the metropolis as a source of corruption and vice.

London comes on apace [Gilpin writes], and all those disgusting ideas, with which its great avenues abound—brick-kilns steaming with offensive smoke—sewers and ditches sweating with filth—heaps of collected soil, and stinks of every denomination—clouds of dust, rising and vanishing from agitated wheels, pursuing each other in

[1] *Jane Austen's Letters*, ed. R. W. Chapman, 'Notes', Addenda.
[2] *Ibid.* pp. 298, 504.
[3] *Observations on the Mountains and Lakes of Cumberland and Westmorland*, sect. xxxii, vol. ii, pp. 263–4.

rapid motion—or taking stationary possession of the road, by becoming the atmosphere of some cumbersome, slow-moving waggon
—villages without rural ideas—trees, and hedge-rows without a
tinge of green—and fields and meadows without pasturage, in which
lowing bullocks are crowded together, waiting for the shambles; or
cows penned, like hogs, to feed on grains.—It was an agreeable
relief to get through this succession of noisome objects, which did
violence to all the senses by turns: and to leave behind us *the busy
hum of men*; stealing from it through the quiet lanes of Surry; which
leading to no great mart, or general rendezvous, afford calmer re-
treats on every side, than can easily be found in the neighbourhood
of so great a town.[1]

Gilpin was joined in his appreciation of the beauties of Surrey
by George Mason whose *An Essay on Design in Gardening* was
first published in 1768. 'When I travel through Surrey',
George Mason wrote, 'and cast my eyes for miles together
(between Leatherhead and Dorking) on the hills and dales, and
beautiful intermixture of lawn wood thicket and grove in the
enclosure of Norbury, can I have the least hesitation in agreeing
with Mr Walpole, that our country is a *school of landscape*?'[2]
This is the world to which Gilpin, Vicar of Boldre, in the New
Forest, and Prebendary of Salisbury, belongs. Surrey is also,
of course, the county in which the action of *Emma* takes place
and Emma remarks to Mrs Elton, 'When you have seen more
of this country, I am afraid you will think you have over-rated
Hartfield. Surry is full of beauties'. To which Mrs Elton replies,
'Oh! yes, I am quite aware of that. It is the garden of England,
you know. Surry is the garden of England.'[3] Emma retorts
that many counties had been called the garden of England, as
well as Surrey.

In the 'Explanation of the Prints' which concludes the
second volume of the *Observations on the Mountains and Lakes of
Cumberland and Westmorland*, there is an example of the rather
pedantic detail of the cult of the picturesque which the novelist
used to provide a satirical, comic undertone. Gilpin explains

[1] *Ibid.* pp. 267–8.
[2] George Mason, *An Essay on Design in Gardening* (London, 1795), p. 143.
[3] *Emma*, chapter 32.

the principles of grouping and the way in which one of the prints illustrates them. Then he remarks:

These two prints are meant to explain the doctrine of grouping larger *cattle*. *Two* will hardly combine. There is indeed no way of forming *two* into a group, but by *uniting* them, as they are represented in the former of these prints. If they stand apart, whatever their attitudes, or situation may be, there will be a deficiency.

But with *three*, you are almost sure of a good group, except indeed they all stand in the same attitude, and at equal distances. They generally however combine the most beautifully, when two are *united*, and the third a little *removed*.

Four introduce a new difficulty in grouping. *Separate* they would have a bad effect. Two, and two together would be equally bad. The only way, in which they will group well, is to *unite three*, as represented in the second of these prints, and to *remove the fourth*.[1]

At the end of chapter 10 of *Pride and Prejudice*, Elizabeth and Mrs Hurst meet Miss Bingley and Darcy. Mrs Hurst then takes Darcy's disengaged arm, and leaves Elizabeth to walk by herself: 'The path just admitted three', and Elizabeth 'who had not the least inclination to remain with them, laughingly answered, "No, no; stay where you are.—You are charmingly group'd, and appear to uncommon advantage. The picturesque would be spoilt by admitting a fourth".'[2] Only the expert on the picturesque would see this joke, and Darcy, Miss Bingley and Mrs Hurst are certainly not meant to see it. The wit here has an irreverence about it which prepares one for the later devastating snub which Elizabeth is to administer when Darcy proposes to her. Mr Hurst himself is described as 'an indolent man, who lived only to eat, drink and play at cards', and the satire therefore gains additional force in so far as it refers to his wife.

Scotland was usually a polite euphemism for Gretna Green, so far as Jane Austen was concerned, as Dr R. W. Chapman has pointed out.[3] But in *Love and Freindship*, Augusta tells Laura 'that having a considerable taste for the Beauties of Nature, her

---

[1] *Observations on the Mountains and Lakes of Cumberland and Westmorland*, 'Explanation of the Prints', vol. II, p. 259.
[2] *Pride and Prejudice*, chapter 10.
[3] See *Northanger Abbey* and *Persuasion*, Index, 'Of Real Places', p. 310.

curiosity to behold the delightful scenes it exhibited in that part of the World had been so much raised by Gilpin's Tour to the Highlands, that she had prevailed on her Father to undertake a Tour to Scotland and had persuaded Lady Dorothea to accompany them'.[1] At the conclusion of Laura's final letter, she tells Marianne how 'I took up my Residence in a romantic Village in the Highlands of Scotland where I have ever since continued, and where I can uninterrupted by unmeaning Visits, indulge in a melancholy solitude, my unceasing Lamentations for the Death of my Father, my Mother, my Husband and my Freind'.[2]

The mock justification of Henry VIII in Jane Austen's *The History of England* is probably another satirical glance at Gilpin's over-enthusiasm for landscape:

Nothing can be said in his vindication [Jane Austen says], but that his abolishing Religious Houses and leaving them to the ruinous depredations of time has been of infinite use to the landscape of England in general, which probably was a principal motive for his doing it, since otherwise why should a Man who was of no Religion himself be at so much trouble to abolish one which had for ages been established in the Kingdom.[3]

Gilpin, as Elizabeth Jenkins has noted,[4] had mentioned Gothic ruins as an example of the many different kinds of picturesque beauty to be found in England; she also pointed out that 'Gilpin's observations on Forest Scenery are plainly glanced at in *Sense and Sensibility*'.[5]

The main authority on Italian landscape in eighteenth-century England observed that 'Jane Austen makes the sensible Elinor an artist, while her emotional sister is merely an admirer of the picturesque. It is notable that Marianne finds Edward's lack of enthusiasm for pictures almost a damning fault.'[6] It is

[1] *Love and Freindship*, Jane Austen, *Minor Works*, p. 105.
[2] *Ibid.* pp. 108–9.
[3] Jane Austen, *Minor Works*, 'The History of England', p. 143.
[4] Elizabeth Jenkins, *Jane Austen*, A Biography (London, 1949), p. 50.
[5] *Ibid.*
[6] Elizabeth Wheeler Manwaring, *Italian Landscape in Eighteenth Century England* (Oxford, 1925), p. 91.

further pointed out that 'Jane Austen's *Emma* painted unsuccessful portraits and presumably landscapes.... Of her most delightful heroines only Catherine Morland is without a native taste for views; and she acquires one with suspicious ease and readiness.'[1]

The cult of the picturesque was a part of the new religion of nature. 'Sir George Beaumont, famous amateur on landscape, painting, and later patron and friend of William Wordsworth, knew Gilpin personally and admired his work immensely.... The record has been printed of a considerable visit that Sir George paid Gilpin at Vicar's Hill, in 1795.'[2] In *Sense and Sensibility*, the sensible but prosaic Edward Ferrars remarks to Marianne that

I have no knowledge in the picturesque, and I shall offend you by my ignorance and want of taste if we come to particulars. I shall call hills steep, which ought to be bold; surfaces strange and uncouth, which ought to be irregular and rugged; and distant objects out of sight, which ought only to be indistinct through the soft medium of a hazy atmosphere.... It exactly answers my idea of a fine country, because it unites beauty with utility—and I dare say it is a picturesque one too, because you admire it; I can easily believe it to be full of rocks and promontories, grey moss and brush wood, but these are all lost on me. I know nothing of the picturesque.[3]

Even Marianne admits that 'admiration of landscape scenery is become a mere jargon. Every body pretends to feel and tries to describe with the taste and elegance of him who first defined what picturesque beauty was.'[4] To this, Edward replies that he likes the fine prospect, but not on picturesque principles: 'I do not like ruined, tattered cottages. I am not fond of nettles, or thistles, or heath blossoms. I have more pleasure in a snug farm-house than a watch-tower—and a troop of tidy, happy villagers please me better than the finest banditti in the world.'[5]

Another reference to the picturesque occurs in *Northanger*

---

[1] Elizabeth Wheeler Manwaring, *op. cit.* pp. 221–2.

[2] William D. Templeman, *The Life and Work of William Gilpin* (University of Illinois Press, 1939), p. 233.

[3] *Sense and Sensibility*, chapter 18.   [4] *Ibid.*   [5] *Ibid.*

Abbey. Here one can see that Jane Austen was interested in the subject herself and knew a great deal about it, though she views enthusiasm on this subject, as on any other, with a certain ironical detachment. The Tilneys are described, 'viewing the country with the eyes of persons accustomed to drawing, and decided on its capability of being formed into pictures, with all the eagerness of real taste'.[1] When the heroine Catherine

confessed and lamented her want of knowledge...a lecture on the picturesque immediately followed, in which his instructions were so clear that she soon began to see beauty in everything admired by him, and her attention was so earnest, that he became perfectly satisfied of her having a great deal of natural taste. He talked of fore-grounds, distances, and second distances—side-screens and perspectives—lights and shades; and Catherine was so hopeful a scholar, that when they gained the top of Beechen Cliff, she voluntarily rejected the whole city of Bath, as unworthy to make part of a landscape. Delighted with her progress, and fearful of wearying her with too much wisdom at once, Henry suffered the subject to decline, and by an easy transition from a piece of rocky fragment and the withered oak which he had placed near its summit, to oaks in general, to forests, the inclosure of them, waste lands, crown lands and government, he shortly found himself arrived at politics; and from politics it was an easy step to silence.[2]

Gilpin's *Observations on the Western Parts of England, relative chiefly to Picturesque Beauty. To which are added, a few remarks on the picturesque beauties of the isle of Wight* was published in 1798, and dedicated to the Right Honourable Henry Addington, Speaker of the House of Commons, an indication of the author's increasing self-confidence, recognition and prestige. Early in the first volume, there is a description of 'the boast of Surrey, the celebrated Box-hill', which almost certainly was in Jane Austen's mind when she placed the climax of her greatest novel in this well-known beauty-spot. Gilpin describes 'its shivering precipices, and downy hillocks, every where interspersed with the mellow verdure of box, which is here and there tinged, as box commonly is, with red and orange'.[3] In Jane Austen, the

---

[1] *Northanger Abbey*, chapter 14.   [2] *Ibid.*
[3] *Observations on the Western Parts of England...* (London, 1798), sect. II, pp. 11–12.

picturesque characteristics of the scene are subordinate to the dramatic tension and explosion which develop, though there is a reference to a moment of quiet, with Emma sitting alone 'in tranquil observation of the beautiful views beneath her'.[1] This is immediately followed by Mr Knightley's brief, devastating rebuke of her rudeness to Miss Bates.

Observations on the coasts of Hampshire, Sussex, and Kent, relative chiefly to picturesque beauty: made in the summer of the year 1774 contains a description of Portsmouth and its environs which bears a similar kind of relationship to the scenes in the third volume of *Mansfield Park*. Jane Austen describes how Mrs Price 'took her weekly walk on the ramparts every fine Sunday throughout the year',[2] and on the Sunday when she, her family, Fanny and Mr Crawford go for a walk after the church service,

The day was uncommonly lovely. It was really March; but it was April in its mild air, brisk, soft wind, and bright sun, occasionally clouded for a minute; and everything looked so beautiful under the influence of such a sky, the effects of the shadows pursuing each other, on the ships at Spithead and the island beyond, with the ever-varying hues of the sea now at high water, dancing in its glee and dashing against the ramparts with so fine a sound, produced altogether such a combination of charms for Fanny, as made her gradually almost careless of the circumstances under which she felt them.[3]

This is a scene of picturesque beauty, appreciated as one would expect of an admirer of Gilpin. In *Persuasion*, there is an enthusiastic description of the beauties of Lyme Regis and its surroundings, 'where a scene so wonderful and so lovely is exhibited, as may more than equal any of the resembling scenes of the far-famed Isle of Wight'.[4] In Gilpin's account of the view of Portsmouth and its environs from Portsdown hill, he mentions how 'beyond all appeared the Isle of Wight; the high grounds of which bounded the prospect. The whole view from Portsdown-hill was picturesque, as well as amusing. The parts were rather large indeed, but they were distinct and well-

<hr/>

[1] *Emma*, chapter 43.
[3] *Ibid.*
[2] *Mansfield Park*, chapter 42.
[4] *Persuasion*, chapter 11.

connected.'[1] The various elements in the scene 'form altogether a very grand assemblage of objects'.[2]

Though Jane Austen both refers to and quotes from Thomson's *Seasons*,[3] the original source of much of the later interest in landscape and the picturesque, it does not appear that she had read the writers who were contemporary with Gilpin, such as Uvedale Price[4] and the poet Richard Payne Knight.[5] On the other hand, she mentions in *Mansfield Park* Humphrey Repton, the notorious improver and author of *Observations on the Theory and Practice of Landscape Gardening* (1803), who is admired by the foolish Mr Rushworth. Jane Austen's use of this aspect of the landscape arts and the picturesque has been dealt with by E. W. Manwaring, who observes, 'Jane Austen's world is much interested in grounds. John Dashwood improved his; and Cleveland, the Palmers' place, offers to Marianne Dashwood, a Grecian temple on an eminence, from which she may survey the prospect toward the horizon hills.'[6]

Art critics such as Ruskin and Sir Kenneth Clark have maintained the general reader's interest in the problem of the transformation of landscape into art. So far as the novel is concerned, perhaps the most significant comment has come from a novelist hostile to Jane Austen. D. H. Lawrence described her as 'mean' and said 'this old maid typifies "personality" instead of character, the sharp knowing in apartness instead of knowing in togetherness, and she is, to my feeling, thoroughly unpleasant, English in the bad, mean, snobbish sense of the word, just as Fielding is English in the good generous sense'.[7]

---

[1] *Observations on the coasts of Hampshire, Sussex, and Kent* . . . (London, 1804), sect. II, p. 15.   [2] *Ibid.* sect. III, p. 21.

[3] Edward Ferrars says that if Marianne had money she would buy up all the copies of Thomson, Cowper and Scott, to prevent them falling into unworthy hands (*Sense and Sensibility*, chapter 17). Catherine Morland learns from Thomson that 'It is a delightful task,/ To teach the young idea how to shoot' (*Northanger Abbey*, chapter 1).   [4] Author of *An Essay on the Picturesque* (1794).

[5] Author of *The Landscape* (1794). See *The Picturesque* by Christopher Hussey (London, 1927).

[6] *Italian Landscape in Eighteenth Century England* (Oxford, 1925), p. 221.

[7] *A Propos of Lady Chatterley's Lover*, reprinted in *Sex, Literature and Censorship*, ed. Harry T. Moore (London, 1955), pp. 265–6.

Whether one agrees with D. H. Lawrence or not, his comments on landscape suggest with brilliant imaginative insight why it has fascinated the English, in general, and such a type of English artist as Jane Austen, in particular. In 'Introduction to these Paintings', after the challenging comment that Blake 'is the only painter of imaginative pictures, apart from landscape that England has produced', Lawrence continues:

Landscape, however, is different. Here the English exist and hold their own. But, for me, personally, landscape is always waiting for something to occupy it. Landscape seems to be *meant* as a background to an intenser vision of life, so to my feeling painted landscape is background with the real subject left out.... It doesn't call up the more powerful responses of the human imagination, the sensual, passional responses. Hence it is the favourite modern form of expression in painting. There is no deep conflict. The instinctive and intuitional consciousness is called into play, but lightly, superficially.... Hence the English have delighted in landscape, and have succeeded in it well. It is a form of escape for them.[1]

---

[1] D. H. Lawrence, 'Introduction to these Paintings', *Phoenix* (London, 1961), p. 561.

CHAPTER 4

DRAMA AND POETRY

In discussing the importance of conversation in Jane Austen's novels, it has been noted how they are naturally dramatic.[1] There is one typically dramatic scene which has been dealt with in an almost identical manner by Fielding, Jane Austen, and George Eliot. It is a kind of 'set-piece' in English fiction—the moment when two ladies who are enemies meet to discuss the gentleman concerned. It is, inevitably, a theatrical moment, and it is interesting that the three novelists, writing at widely separated intervals of time, should have adopted a very similar method. The example in Fielding occurs in *Joseph Andrews*, book IV, chapter VI, where Lady Booby and Pamela discuss the former's nephew. Fielding, of course, like so many novelists in the eighteenth century, was also a dramatist, and in such a description as this, there is the dramatist's instinctive appreciation of an effective scene. But the tone, accent, and manner of writing are also familiar. They bring to mind, in particular, the conversation between Elinor and Lucy Steele in *Sense and Sensibility* which occurs in the first chapter of the second volume (chapter 23). In Jane Austen, the division of the novels into volumes suggests a parallel with the acts of a play, but here the actual setting is also dramatic, like Fielding's. A comparable moment takes place in *Middlemarch*, book III, chapter XXXI, where Mrs Bulstrode calls to inquire about the seriousness of Rosamond Vincy's relationship with Lydgate.

Pamela, Lucy Steele, and Rosamond Vincy resemble each other in their feline natures. They are types of character which the female novelist naturally excels in depicting. One notes how much more effective the scene is, as rendered by Jane Austen and George Eliot. Being put in terms of dialogue

---

[1] See Chapter 2, 'Moralists in Prose', p. 48 above.

instead of reported speech, the accent is more vividly presented, more directly caught. The tension of the moment is, however, similarly heightened in each of the examples of feminine swordsmanship. The concentration on minor points of detail, in each of the dramatic situations, suggests the emotional conflict underneath the calm surface of the conversation as effectively as if the characters were acting (as in a sense they are) on a stage. We even follow the movements of their eyes. In Fielding and Jane Austen the enemies are on terms of equality, and their glances never meet—'Whilst both contemplated their own faces, they paid a cross compliment to each other's charms' and 'the two fair rivals were thus seated side by side at the same table, and with the utmost harmony engaged in forwarding the same work'. In George Eliot, Mrs Bulstrode is in a position of some authority over Rosamond, and so her eyes ('which were rather fine') can, after the necessary preliminaries, finally come to rest on Rosamond's, who blushes.

Scenes of this nature are frequent in the novels of Henry James. Novels of satirical comedy, implying a civilized standard of personal relationships, tend to be dramatic in this manner. The quality and tone of such writing constitute a great strength, not only in the novels of Jane Austen, but in much of the finer part of English fiction as a whole. In replacing the drama, the novel absorbed some of its finer qualities, in the realm of comedy, at least.

Jane Austen's interest in poetry and drama may partly explain the comparative sensitiveness of her prose, and her ability to select and concentrate when dealing with intense situations and moments. In drama, her tastes were catholic, as they were in the novel. When the possibility of acting a play is being discussed at Mansfield Park, John Home's *Douglas* and Edward Moore's *The Gamester* are mentioned, together with *Hamlet*, *Macbeth* and *Othello*, as tragedies; Sheridan's *The Rivals* and *The School for Scandal*, Cumberland's *The Wheel of Fortune* and George Colman the younger's *The Heir at Law*, as comedies. The play that is actually performed (*Lovers' Vows*, Mrs Inchbald's translation from the German of Kotzebue), and its relevance to the story of the novel, have already received a good deal of attention.[1] That Jane Austen read and enjoyed literature of little permanent interest is obvious. Yet a knowledge of Shakespeare, too, is taken for granted. In *Mansfield Park*, Fanny Price's reading of *Henry VIII* to Lady Bertram is interrupted, ironically enough, by Henry Crawford. It is Wolsey's farewell speech that he interrupts and completes:

his reading was capital, and her pleasure in good reading extreme. To *good* reading, however, she had been long used; her uncle read well—her cousins all—Edmund very well; but in Mr Crawford's reading there was a variety of excellence beyond what she had ever met with. The King, the Queen, Buckingham, Wolsey, Cromwell, all were given in turn; for with the happiest knack, the happiest power of jumping and guessing, he could always light, at will, on the best scene, or the best speeches of each; and whether it were dignity or pride, or tenderness or remorse, or whatever were to be expressed, he could do it with equal beauty.—It was truly dramatic. —His acting had first taught Fanny what pleasure a play might give, and his reading brought all his acting before her again.[2]

No doubt, there is a certain autobiographical element here, and Jane Austen is recalling the family amateur theatricals of her youth. But there is also an ironical undertone. Henry Crawford himself is something of an actor in actual life. He, like Wolsey, is shortly to put forth 'the tender leaves of hope' and bear his blushing honours thick upon him only to fall immediately to ruin, 'never to hope again'.[3]

Henry Crawford says that he does not think that he has had a volume of Shakespeare in his hand since he was fifteen. 'But Shakespeare one gets acquainted with without knowing how. It is a part of an Englishman's constitution.' Even the serious Edmund remarks that one is familiar with Shakespeare from

---

[1] See E. M. Butler, '*Mansfield Park* and Kotzebue's *Lovers' Vows*', *The Modern Language Review* (July 1933), with 'A Reply' by H. Winifred Husbands (April 1934). Also see William Reitzel, '*Mansfield Park* and *Lovers' Vows*', *Review of English Studies* (October 1933).

[2] *Mansfield Park*, chapter 34.

[3] *Henry VIII*, Act III, scene 2, ll. 351–78 (*The Complete Works of William Shakespeare*, ed. W. J. Craig, Oxford, 1905).

one's earliest years. 'We all talk Shakespeare, use his similies, and describe with his descriptions.' He is universally known in bits and scraps and frequently known pretty thoroughly. Henry Crawford has the unusual gift of being able to read him well aloud, according to Edmund. The conversation now passes to a discussion of the importance of reading the liturgy and sermons as if to underline the fact that that is Edmund's vocation and to contrast him with his theatrical rival.

In *Sense and Sensibility*, Mrs Dashwood takes up a volume of Shakespeare, at one point of the story, and remarks to Marianne that Willoughby had gone away before they had been able to complete the reading of *Hamlet*. Darcy, too, refers indirectly to this play: 'There is, I believe, in every disposition a tendency to some particular evil, a natural defect, which not even the best education can overcome.'[1] Hamlet's remarks, from which Darcy's derive, reflect general Elizabethan theories concerning human character and behaviour:

> So, oft it chances in particular men,
> That for some vicious mole of nature in them,
> As, in their birth,—wherein they are not guilty,
> Since nature cannot choose his origin,—
> By the o'ergrowth of some complexion,
> Oft breaking down the pales and forts of reason,
> Or by some habit that too much o'er-leavens
> The form of plausive manners; that these men,
> Carrying, I say, the stamp of one defect,
> Being nature's livery, or fortune's star,
> Their virtues else, be they as pure as grace,
> As infinite as man may undergo,
> Shall in the general censure take corruption
> From that particular fault: the dram of eale
> Doth all the noble substance of a doubt,
> To his own scandal.[2]

Here, as in the case of Henry Crawford, there is an element of unconscious irony. For the viciousness of Darcy is due to his birth and his mistaken pride in his rank, and he has to learn to

[1] *Pride and Prejudice*, chapter 11.   [2] *Hamlet*, Act I, scene 4, ll. 23–38.

eradicate this defect. The element of evil in Darcy mars and flaws the essential nobility of his nature, and leads to a scandalous impropriety of behaviour. The psychology that lies behind Darcy's self-criticism can be traced back through the eighteenth-century doctrine of the prevailing passion, familiar through Pope's *An Essay on Man*, to Jonson's theory of the humours, reflected in Hamlet's speech.

Generally speaking, Shakespeare's poetic drama was too complex, and too different a medium from Jane Austen's essentially prosaic art, for her to be able to make direct use of it. However, when Catherine Morland was in training for a heroine, between the ages of fifteen and seventeen, 'from Shakespeare she gained a great store of information'.[1] What she gains is a series of commonplace reflections and clichés, such as a description of the young woman in love always looking like Patience on a monument smiling at Grief. Yet Jane Austen seems to have repented of her sarcastic allusion to Shakespeare's sentimental image. For in her final completed novel, *Persuasion*, the climax occurs during a discussion between Anne Elliot and Captain Harville on the subject of women's constancy, which follows the lines of the debate between Viola and the Duke in *Twelfth Night*.

The heroines of Shakespeare's comedies and of Jane Austen's novels are equally witty, but Shakespeare's Rosalind, Viola and Beatrice have beneath the surface, verbal wit of their prose speech an emotional depth which finds its natural utterance in poetry. Jane Austen was no poet. Her strength and subtlety is in implying, analysing and leading up to the direct expression of emotion, rather than in expressing emotion itself. Indeed, the direct expression of feeling is, for her, usually a sign of bad taste, as in *Sense and Sensibility*, and it is only at the end of her novels that she allows her lovers to confess to each other— Darcy's premature proposal being an exception, but essentially different from the mutual confession of love with which the novels end. In *Emma*, the wit of the heroine and the silence of

[1] *Northanger Abbey*, chapter i.

the hero are the means by which they escape the emotional involvement with each other which would otherwise develop. Emma's wit reminds one at times of Millamant, and when, towards the end of the novel she is described as being 'faultless in spite of all her faults',[1] Jane Austen repeats the words of Mirabell in Congreve's *The Way of the World*: 'I like her with all her faults; nay, I like her for her faults. Her follies are so natural, or so artful, that they become her; and those affectations which in another woman would be odious, serve but to make her more agreeable.'[2]

The historian of English comic drama during the first half of the eighteenth century concludes his survey with the remark that 'The comedy of the century, so far as it was a homogeneous movement like Elizabethan and Restoration comedy, was never more than second-rate'.[3] In *Mansfield Park*, the plays that are considered, apart from Shakespeare, are very inferior. Moreover, manners had changed rapidly, so that a play such as George Colman the elder's *The Clandestine Marriage*, originally produced in 1766, and seen by Jane Austen herself in 1813,[4] was considered out of date by Mrs Inchbald in the prefatory remarks to the printed edition:

Lord Ogleby, once the most admired part in this comedy, is an evidence of the fluctuation of manners, modes, and opinions:—forty years ago, it was reckoned so natural a representation of a man of fashion, that several noblemen were said to have been in the author's thoughts when he designed the character: now, no part is so little understood in the play; and his foibles seem so discordant with the manly faults of the present time, that his good qualities cannot atone for them.[5]

Even Sheridan seems to have had hardly any direct influence on the novel, except in so far as the illiteracy of Mrs Malaprop may have provided a hint for Miss Bates and Lydia Languish

---

[1] *Emma*, chapter 49.   [2] Act I, scene 3.
[3] F. W. Bateson, *English Comic Drama, 1700–1750* (Oxford, 1929), p. 151.
[4] *Jane Austen's Letters*, ed. R. W. Chapman, p. 338.
[5] G. Colman the elder, *The Clandestine Marriage*, with remarks by Mrs Inchbald (London), p. 5 (undated).

for Lydia Bennet.[1] Goldsmith, who was one of Jane Austen's favourite writers, did not provide her with characters or a plot that she could use, though when Mr Hardcastle remarks in *She Stoops to Conquer*, Act 1, scene 1, 'I love every thing that's old: old friends, old times, old manners, old books, old wine', he reminds one of Mr Woodhouse's similar affection for everything that is old.

Poetry, in the Augustan tradition, was more suited to Jane Austen's needs. Her nephew has stated that 'She thoroughly enjoyed Crabbe; perhaps on account of a certain resemblance to herself in minute and highly finished detail; and would sometimes say, in jest, that, if she ever married at all, she could fancy being Mrs Crabbe.... Scott's poetry gave her great pleasure'.[2] In *Sense and Sensibility*, the contemporary fashionable tastes in poetry are mockingly described by Elinor after Willoughby has called on Marianne. She ironically suggests that Marianne has 'already ascertained Mr Willoughby's opinion in almost every matter of importance. You know what he thinks of Cowper and Scott; you are certain of his estimating their beauties as he ought, and you have received every assurance of his admiring Pope no more than is proper.'[3]

Pope's *Elegy to the Memory of an Unfortunate Lady* is referred to ironically in *Northanger Abbey* as one of the poems that the aspiring heroine must learn, and the hypocritical Mr Elliot in *Persuasion* quotes from the *Essay on Criticism*,[4] which is also misquoted in the letters, with the comment 'There has been one infallible Pope in the world'.[5] A comic adaptation of a line in *An Essay on Man* is made in one of the early skits.[6] Though Jane Austen is usually considered to be anti-romantic, her attitude to the greatest of the poets of the Augustan age is one of

---

[1] This latter influence was pointed out by E. E. Phare in *Notes and Queries* (May 1964) together with the satire on Dr Fordyce by Sheridan as well as by Jane Austen. See above, chapter 2, 'Moralists in Prose', p. 27, n. 2.

[2] James Edward Austen-Leigh, *Memoir of Jane Austen*, ed. R. W. Chapman (Oxford, 1951), pp. 89–90.

[3] *Sense and Sensibility*, chapter 10. [4] *Persuasion*, chapter 16.

[5] *Jane Austen's Letters*, ed. R. W. Chapman, p. 362.

[6] Jane Austen, *Minor Works*, p. 154.

detachment. Yet there can be no doubt that she owed much to him for her general ideas about self-love, reason, the passions, the predominant passions, instinct, happiness, the characters of men and women, the use of riches, and the various kinds of stupidity to be found in society. The delicacy and refinement of the satire in *The Rape of the Lock* must have appealed to her. The airy and ingenious mockery of false appearances and of heroism was the mode in which they both excelled. 'New things are made familiar, and familiar things are made new', Dr Johnson remarked of *The Rape of the Lock*. Pope's poetry exemplifies the power of the imagination, as defined by Coleridge, and it is this same gift in the artist which illuminates the surface realism of Jane Austen's novels. Other characteristics of Pope's poetry noted by Dr Johnson were technical prudence, uniformity, systematical arrangement, power of selection and combination, independence, avoidance of haste, integrity, elegance and simplicity. These are also to be found in Jane Austen's fiction. The minute and punctilious observation, the indefatigable diligence of the revisions were also noted by Dr Johnson, and it is for such reasons that the art of Jane Austen merits praise. Moreover, the moral foundation of her satire is Augustan. The justification of her destructive criticism of society is what Pope summed up as 'the strong Antipathy of Good to Bad'.[1] Ridicule is for Pope a 'sacred weapon! left for Truth's defence',[2] and Jane Austen agreed with Dr Johnson that 'the basis of all excellence is truth'.[3]

Dr Johnson's criticism of life in his two major poems, *London* and *The Vanity of Human Wishes*, was, no doubt, agreeable to Jane Austen, but Crabbe's stories in verse and descriptions were more congenial to her. His poems, *The Village* (1783), *The Parish Register* (1807), *The Borough* (1810) and *Tales* (1812) are partly concerned with the poorest classes of society, but they also contain stories of middle-class life. Some of the tales are tragic, while the comedies, ironical appreciations of human

---

[1] *Epilogue to the Satires*, Dialogue II, l. 198.　　[2] *Ibid.* l. 212.
[3] *Lives of the English Poets*, 'Life of Cowley'.

folly and vice, are told with verve, terseness and pungency. In *The Village*, Crabbe says that he will avoid poetical descriptions of groves and happy valleys, and

> paint the Cot,
> As Truth will paint it, and as Bards will not:

Occasionally Jane Austen seems to be directly indebted to Crabbe for certain details: in *The Parish Register*, Part II, there is a Fanny Price, and in *The Borough*, Letter VII, there is a reference to a 'lucky guess' which may have suggested Emma's use of this phrase. But more generally the resemblance between Crabbe and Jane Austen is a question of tone and accent and the objects of their satire. Jane Austen satirized sentiment and the horror-terror story in *Sense and Sensibility* and *Northanger Abbey*. Crabbe reacts against them in a similar way in *The Borough*, Letter XX, the story of Ellen Orford:

> I've often marvel'd, when by night, by day,
> I've mark'd the manners moving in my way,
> And heard the language and beheld the lives
> Of lass and lover, goddesses and wives,
> That books, which promise much of life to give,
> Should show so little how we truly live.[1]

Crabbe speaks of the middle class of society in similar terms to those of Mrs West:[2] 'It is in this class of mankind that more originality of character, more variety of fortune, will be met with; because, on the one hand, they do not live in the eye of the world, and therefore are not kept in awe by the dread of observation and indecorum; neither, on the other, are they debarred by their want of means from the cultivation of mind and the pursuits of wealth and ambition.'[3] Jane Austen and Crabbe do not always confine themselves to this world, but the moral standards they bring to bear on life reflect the finer consciousness of the class to which they belong. They judge

---

[1] *The Borough*, Letter XX. [2] See above, p. 43.
[3] Quoted by René Huchon in *George Crabbe and His Times* (London, 1907), pp. 258-9.

their own society by its own best standards, and in dealing with poorer or wealthier classes than their own, the same values are evoked.

Jane Austen took from Crabbe what he had to give her in content, tone, wit, attitudes and points of view, as she did from other writers. One cannot, however, identify or compare, at length or in detail, her art with his. The subtlety of her relationship with other writers is in its indirectness, the pattern that emerges from a variety of influences, a pattern that is not in any way inconsistent with an effect of complete spontaneity and originality.

Though the bases of Jane Austen's art were Augustan and eighteenth century, she was not completely out of sympathy with the new romanticism. 'When I look out on such a night as this', Fanny Price remarks, 'I feel that there could be neither wickedness nor sorrow in the world; and there certainly would be less of both if the sublimity of nature were more attended to, and people were carried more out of themselves by contemplating such a scene.'[1] Fanny Price recalls *The Merchant of Venice*: at Belmont, 'the moon shines bright', as Lorenzo and Jessica speak of Troilus, Thisbe, Dido, Medea, and themselves.[2] The 'enthusiasm' of Fanny Price for nature, however, is also influenced by Gilpin and Wordsworth, and has an austerity that is lacking in the more direct emotionalism of Shakespeare. It was 'a beautiful evening, mild and still', when Fanny Price and the rest of the party drove back from Sotherton.[3] Wordsworth had written 'It is a beauteous evening calm and free' when he composed his sonnet on the beach at Calais, and it is possible that the novelist and the poet (or his sister) remembered a passage in Ann Radcliffe's *The Mysteries of Udolpho*, where the same phrase is used, in a similar context.[4]

Other poets mentioned by Jane Austen, such as Burns, Scott and Byron did not have the same intimate connections with her

---

[1] *Mansfield Park*, chapter 11. [2] *The Merchant of Venice*, Act v, scene 1.
[3] *Mansfield Park*, chapter 10.
[4] *The Mysteries of Udolpho* (Everyman's Library), vol. ii, p. 254.

central interests as Wordsworth and eighteenth-century nature poetry, and do not seem to have had any deep influence on her, though she was surprisingly tolerant towards new trends. Apart from the novel, her three favourite writers appear to have been Dr Johnson, Crabbe and Cowper, in that order of priority, three men of essentially religious outlook whose influence would strengthen the tendencies encouraged by the home in which she was brought up.

Finally, Jane Austen's knowledge of Italian would, presumably, be sufficient to allow her to translate operatic arias, as Anne Elliot does in *Persuasion*, and she may have read *The Inferno* of Dante in Cary's translation (1805) and *The Purgatorio* and *The Paradiso* (1812). Through the preface to Crabbe's *Tales* (1812) she would have at least heard of Chaucer. It is unlikely that she had a first-hand acquaintance with Langland's *Piers Plowman*, though Whitaker's edition of the 'C' text appeared in 1813, and she may have heard the outlines of the story in her youth or read references to it later.

In *Persuasion*, Captain Benwick is described as a young man of considerable taste in reading, though principally in poetry. He and Anne discuss *Marmion*, *The Lady of the Lake*, *The Giaour*, and *The Bride of Abydos*:

he shewed himself so intimately acquainted with all the tenderest songs of the one poet, and all the impassioned descriptions of hopeless agony of the other; he repeated, with such tremulous feeling, the various lines which imaged a broken heart, or a mind destroyed by wretchedness, and looked so entirely as if he meant to be understood, that she ventured to hope he did not always read only poetry; and to say, that she thought it was the misfortune of poetry, to be seldom safely enjoyed by those who enjoyed it completely; and that the strong feelings which alone could estimate it truly, were the very feelings which ought to taste it but sparingly.[1]

Anne recommends a larger allowance of prose in his daily study, mentioning 'such works of our best moralists, such collections of the finest letters, such memoirs of characters of worth and

---

[1] *Persuasion*, chapter 11.

suffering, as occurred to her at the moment as calculated to rouse and fortify the mind by the highest precepts, and the strongest examples of moral and religious endurances'. Anne's views on the dangers involved in too much reading of romantic poetry and the importance of counteracting such emotional indulgence by means of extensive reading of prose, no doubt, reflected the ideas and to a certain extent, perhaps, even the experience, of Jane Austen herself.

PART II
THE TRADITION IN THE NOVEL

CHAPTER 5

THE BEGINNINGS

It is unlikely that Jane Austen read any fiction earlier than Bunyan and there are no direct references to *The Pilgrim's Progress* or *The Life and Death of Mr Badman* in her novels or letters. However, she expressed sympathy with the Evangelicals, and the satirical portraits of different types of religious hypocrisy to be found in the two writers are in the same tradition. Dr Johnson, Jane Austen's favourite writer in prose, was reported by Boswell to have praised Bunyan highly: 'His "Pilgrim's Progress" has great merit, both for invention, imagination, and the conduct of the story; and it has had the best evidence of its merit, the general and continued approbation of mankind.'[1] Simple, Sloth, Presumption, Formalist, Mistrust and Timorous have their equivalents in Jane Austen. Mr Brisk, 'a man of some breeding, and that pretended to religion, but a man that stuck very close to the world' who courts Mercy in the second part of *The Pilgrim's Progress* until he learns that she is genuinely interested in the poor, has his equivalent in Mr Elton; Talkative, By-Ends and Ignorance (which, for Bunyan, as for Jane Austen, means spiritual vulgarity rather than intellectual feebleness) in the first part of Bunyan's allegory belong to the realistic world of the novel and are not merely abstractions. Sotherton in *Mansfield Park*, has its By-Path-Meadow, and the heroine her moments of despair in Doubting Castle. Jane Austen's Vanity Fair is judged more tolerantly, but the judgement is made. It is as a satirist, a witty and destructive critic of society who appealed to Swift ('I have been better entertained, and more informed by a Chapter in the *Pilgrim's Progress*, than by a long Discourse upon

[1] Boswell, *Life of Johnson*, The Globe Edition, pp. 260-1.

the *Will* and the *Intellect*, and *simple* or *complex* Ideas'),[1] that
Bunyan is related to Jane Austen. The avarice of Mrs Norris
and the social-climbing of Mr Collins represent a criticism of
religion that Bunyan would have understood. Mr Worldly
Wiseman personifies a point of view with which Jane Austen
had more sympathy than Bunyan, and she has been accused of
mercenary attitudes and an essential materialism, though the
creator of the Crawfords, the Coles in *Emma*, and of Sir Walter
Elliot can hardly be dismissed as a blind worshipper of Mam-
mon. Elinor Dashwood, Edward Ferrars, and Colonel Brandon
in *Sense and Sensibility*, Fanny Price and Edmund Bertram in
Mansfield Park, and Anne Elliot, Nurse Rooke and Mrs Smith
in *Persuasion* embody her positive belief in simple virtue.

Though the satire and irony of Swift remind one of Jane
Austen, his indignation, hatred and violence were too direct and
extreme to make his writings generally of use to her. But they
exploit the same technique of deflation of character and motive,
involving sometimes a partial deception of the reader who is
lured and persuaded to approve of the seemingly good, but
wicked character to the detriment of the misunderstood, or
misrepresented personification of virtue. If Jane Austen is indebted to Swift, it is to the digressions contained in *A Tale of a
Tub*, to *An Argument to prove that the abolishing of Christianity may . . .
be attended with some Inconveniences*, *A Letter to a very Young Lady on
her Marriage*, and *Hints towards an Essay in Conversation* rather
than to *Gulliver's Travels*.

The most moral of English novelists, Samuel Richardson, is
also the least ironical and witty. It was his detailed study of
states of mind and feeling rather than his comparatively crude
treatment of morals, that provided Jane Austen with a model.
Pamela, accepted without irony by Richardson as an embodi-
ment of virtue, supplied hints for the satirical portrayal of Lucy
Steele in *Sense and Sensibility*. Lady Davers, the termagant sister
of Mr B—, resembles Lady Catherine de Bourgh in *Pride and
Prejudice*. When Richardson has to deal with characters from

---

[1] Swift, *A Letter to a Young Gentleman lately enter'd into Holy Orders*.

'high life', his touch fails. In the following conversation between Pamela, Mr B—, and Lady Davers, one notes how the
style of the writing gradually degenerates into melodramatic
fustian: the crudeness of Richardson here needs no emphasizing.
Yet it was such raw material that Jane Austen refined to create
the scenes between Elizabeth Bennet, Mr Darcy, and Lady
Catherine de Bourgh. The difference, of course, also consists in
the fact that Elizabeth Bennet is a gentleman's daughter, and
aware of it. Pamela is much more obsequious:

Not considering anything, I ran out of the closet, and threw myself
at my dear master's feet, as he held her hand, in order to lead her
out; and I said, 'Dearest sir, let me beg, that no act of unkindness,
for my sake, pass between so worthy and so near relations. Dear,
dear madam', said I, and clasped her knees, 'pardon and excuse
the unhappy cause of all this evil; on my knees I beg your ladyship
to receive me to your grace and favour, and you shall find me
incapable of any triumph but in your ladyship's goodness to me.'
  'Creature,' said she, 'art *thou* to beg an excuse for me? Art *thou*
to implore my forgiveness? Is it to *thee* I am to owe the favour, that
I am not cast headlong from my brother's presence? Begone to thy
corner, wench! begone I say, lest thy paramour kill me for trampling
thee under my foot!' 'Rise, my dear Pamela,' said my master;
'rise, dear life of my life; and expose not so much worthiness to the
ungrateful scorn of so violent a spirit.' And so he led me to my
closet again, and there I sat and wept.[1]

Lucy Steele adopts the same tone of ignominious flattery
towards Mrs Ferrars as Pamela does to Lady Davers. The
description given of Lucy Steele's character is perhaps as good
a summary of Pamela as one could hope to find:

the active, contriving manager; uniting at once a desire of smart
appearance with the utmost frugality, and ashamed to be suspected
of half her economical practices; pursuing her own interest in every
thought; courting the favour of Colonel Brandon, Mrs Jennings,
and of every wealthy friend...a most encouraging instance of what
an earnest, an unceasing attention to self-interest, will do in securing
every advantage of fortune, with no other sacrifice than that of time
and conscience.[2]

[1] Richardson, *The Complete Works*, ed. W. M. Lyon Phelps (London, 1902),
Pamela, vol. ii, p. 190. [2] *Sense and Sensibility*, chapters 48 and 50.

By her gratitude for the unkindness she receives, Lucy Steele becomes as necessary to Mrs Ferrars as Pamela does to Lady Davers. The interest in social distinctions, in manners and morals, is common to Richardson and Jane Austen, though the discriminations of the later novelist are so much more delicate as to make the efforts of the pioneer read like a burlesque. But the sentiments of Lady Davers are essentially those of Lady Catherine de Bourgh. The one says: 'Thou'rt almost got into a fool's paradise, I doubt! And wilt find thyself terribly mistaken in a little while, if thou thinkest my brother will disgrace his family to humour thy baby-face!'[1] Lady Catherine de Bourgh is equally violent: 'The upstart pretensions of a young woman without family, connections, or fortune. Is this to be endured? But it must not, shall not be. If you were sensible of your own good, you would not wish to quit the sphere, in which you have been brought up.'[2] The reactions of Pamela and Elizabeth Bennet to the formidable challenge, are, of course, completely different, the one passively retiring to her closet, the other, after utterly annihilating her enemy, politely escorting her to her carriage. The difference in response accords with the difference in social standing of the two characters, and this, in its turn, reflects the widely different interests of the two writers.

Richardson's greatest novel, the tragic *Clarissa*, did not, generally speaking, supply Jane Austen with characters or situations suitable for her kind of satirical comedy, though it may have provided a hint for the scenes of Fanny Price's degradation at Portsmouth in *Mansfield Park*.[3] On the other hand, 'every circumstance narrated in *Sir Charles Grandison*, all that was ever said or done in the cedar parlour was familiar to

[1] Richardson, *The Complete Works*, Pamela, vol. II, p. 146.
[2] *Pride and Prejudice*, chapter 56.
[3] Mr B. C. Southam has recently pointed out similarities between Mr Collins and the Rev. Elias Brand in *Clarissa* (*Notes and Queries*, May 1963). Mrs E. E. Duncan-Jones has traced an allusion to *Clarissa* in Jane Austen's letters (*Notes and Queries*, September 1963), and found a parallel between Mr B—'s proposal to Pamela and Darcy's first declaration (*Notes and Queries*, February 1957), and between the Selby sisters in *Sir Charles Grandison*, and the Steele sisters in *Sense and Sensibility* (*The Times Literary Supplement*, September 10, 1964).

her; and the wedding days of Lady L. and Lady G. were so well remembered as if they had been among living friends'.[1] There is an upstart called Captain Anderson in *Sir Charles Grandison*, who pays court to Harriet Byron's friend, Charlotte Grandison; he might be the model for Willoughby in *Sense and Sensibility* or Wickham in *Pride and Prejudice*. The style of the writing itself, with its subtlety and delicacy of touch, its crispness tending naturally towards epigram, recalls Jane Austen's:

Captain Anderson appeared to me at first a man of sense, as well as an agreeable man in his person and air. He had a lively and easy elocution. He spoke without doubt, and I had therefore the less doubt of his understanding. The man who knows how to say agreeable things to a woman in an agreeable manner has her vanity on his side, since to doubt his veracity would be to question her own merit. When he came to write, my judgement was even still more engaged in his favour than before. But when he thought himself on a safe footing with me, he then lost his handwriting, and his style, and even his orthography.[2]

The theme of the father who is nearly responsible for the ruin of his daughters reminds one of Mr Bennet in *Pride and Prejudice* and of Sir Thomas Bertram in *Mansfield Park*: 'Thus had Sir Thomas Grandison with all his pride like to have thrown his daughter, a woman of high character, fine understanding and an exalted mind, into the arms of a man who had neither fortune nor education, nor yet good sense nor generosity of heart, to countenance his pretensions to such a lady, or her for marrying beneath herself.'[3]

Jane Austen admired Richardson's power of preserving the consistency of his characters, and her knowledge of his works was 'probably such as no one is likely again to acquire'.[4] Yet she could still see his faults. In her unfinished novel *Sanditon*, there is a satirical portrait of a typically enthusiastic admirer of Richardson. Sir Edward Denham had read more sentimental

---

[1] J. E. Austen-Leigh, *Memoir of Jane Austen*, ed. R. W. Chapman (1951), p. 89.
[2] Richardson, *The Complete Works*, *Sir Charles Grandison*, vol. II, Letter xxxv, p. 225.
[3] *Ibid.* vol. II, Letter xxxvi, p. 267.
[4] J. E. Austen-Leigh, *Memoir of Jane Austen*, p. 89.

novels than agreed with him; 'his fancy had been early caught by all the impassioned, & most exceptionable parts of Richardson; & such Authors as have since appeared to tread in Richardson's steps, so far as Man's determined pursuit of Woman in defiance of every opposition of feeling and convenience is concerned'. These works had since 'occupied the greater part of his literary hours, & formed his character'.[1] The result of his addiction is shown in the later part of the story. Jane Austen both appreciated Richardson's virtues and was one of his keenest critics. Her mockery was all the more effective because of its delicacy. She owed much to him, but her six slim major novels also contain the final implied comment on his prolix art with its curious mixture of coarseness and distinction.

The ironical tone and satirical manner of Fielding were more congenial, as has been seen in the comparison of passages from *Joseph Andrews*, *Sense and Sensibility*, and *Middlemarch*.[2] The satire of various kinds of vulgarity in Fielding's novels, his hatred of cant, accompanied by a more virile coarseness than Richardson's prurience allowed, would not be shocking to Jane Austen any more than it was to the much more prim Fanny Burney, but it does not appear that his fiction influenced her directly to any great extent. Realism, burlesque, a fine dramatic sense, command of dialogue, a rudimentary psychology, sentiment, humanity and the 'philosophy of the heart', together with many other characteristics of Jane Austen's own fiction, still did not provide her with a mode, a style, or a set of conventions that she could accept. It was not merely that language, manners and morals had changed, and that Jane Austen was fastidious. Mrs Jennings in *Sense and Sensibility*, John Thorpe in *Northanger Abbey*, and Admiral Croft in *Persuasion*, are vulgar, coarse and virile in the Fielding manner: isolated examples which show that Jane Austen could absorb at least some aspects of the world of Fielding's fiction. She also

[1] Jane Austen, *Minor Works*, 'Sanditon', p. 404.
[2] See above, Chapter 4, 'Drama and Poetry', pp. 69–70.

had a similar appreciation of the frequently hypocritical and mercenary motives of the self-righteous. But Fielding viewed the world as a shrewd, compassionate, classically educated, eighteenth-century gentleman, and the attitude towards it that he depicts is that of the predatory, sexually excited male. There is a sense in which one can justly say that he was, though infinitely more intelligent than Richardson, more simple and comparatively uninterested in the complications of the female heart. Where he most resembles Jane Austen is in his sense of social distinctions, and in short, dramatic, lightly satirical scenes, where his control of nuance and tone in speech resembles Swift's in his less savagely satirical passages. Swift had also an interest in words and language that neither Richardson nor Fielding possessed, but there seems to be no evidence that Jane Austen had read *A Complete Collection of Genteel and Ingenious Conversation*. It was to the women novelists of the eighteenth century who modified and developed the methods of Richardson and Fielding that Jane Austen looked for guidance and example in matters of technique.

CHAPTER 6

THE FEMINIST TRADITION

The feminist tradition in the English novel was well established when Jane Austen began writing, and though not particularly distinguished, the best work embodied a view of life which she could accept as partly valid and relevant. One of the novels that served as a model was Charlotte Lennox's *The Female Quixote*, published in 1752. It is a burlesque of the voluminous seventeenth-century French romances of La Calprenède and Madeleine de Scudéry. In a letter to Cassandra in 1807, Jane Austen describes her disgust on reading the badly translated and indelicate *Alphonsine* of Madame de Genlis, and continues: 'we changed it for the "Female Quixote", which now makes our evening amusement; to me a very high one, as I find the work quite equal to what I remembered it'.[1] Mrs Lennox's satire was obviously one of the important influences inspiring the ridicule of sentiment, horror and terror in *Northanger Abbey*.

The subject of the old romances had been love seen against a heroic background. Mrs Lennox and Jane Austen ridicule the false taste and behaviour caused by reading romances and melodramatic literature. *The Female Quixote* begins with an account of 'some useless additions to a fine lady's education', showing 'the bad effects of a whimsical study, which, some will say, is borrowed from Cervantes'. The theme of education, the mistakes caused by self-deception encouraged by wrong standards and ideals, the attempt to live in accordance with principles that cannot be applied to the world of ordinary, normal personal relationships, lie behind much of Jane Austen's criticism of feminine triviality. An exaggerated idealism is, for her, as dangerous as an extreme cynicism.

Arabella, whose adventures Mrs Lennox describes, has ideas

[1] *Jane Austen's Letters*, ed. R. W. Chapman, p. 173.

similar to those which Isabella Thorpe, who leads the heroine
astray in *Northanger Abbey*, pretends to have:

Her ideas, from the manner of her life, and the objects around her,
had taken a romantic turn; and, supposing romances were real
pictures of life, from them she drew all her notions and expectations.
By them she was taught to believe, that love was the ruling principle
of the world; that every other passion was subordinate to this; and
that it caused all the happiness and miseries of life. Her glass, which
she often consulted, always showed her a form so extremely lovely,
that, not finding herself engaged in such adventures as were common
to the heroines in the romances she read, she often complained of the
insensibility of mankind, upon whom her charms seemed to have so
little influence.[1]

Catherine Morland, the heroine of *Northanger Abbey*, is a
fundamentally sensible girl. Her delusions are temporary, and
soon cured. Jane Austen appears to be stressing this difference
in the early chapters of the novel, where she emphasizes the
complete ordinariness of her heroine, deliberately contrasting
her with the romantic Arabella, whose conceit and egoism Mrs
Lennox makes clear. Arabella's mistaken ideas are based on
self-deception:

The perfect retirement she lived in afforded, indeed, no opportunities of making the conquest she desired; but she could not comprehend how any solitude could be obscure enough to conceal a beauty
like hers from notice: and thought the reputation of her charms
sufficient to bring a crowd of adorers to demand her of her father.
Her mind being wholly filled with the most extravagant expectations, she was alarmed by every trifling incident: and kept in a
continual anxiety by a vicissitude of hopes, fears, wishes and
disappointments.[2]

Whereas Catherine's suspicion that General Tilney is a
wicked intriguer is not wholly untrue, Arabella's credulity
when she allows herself to be persuaded that the gardener is a
great personage who descends to menial service because of love
for her is a stock convention of romance, which Jane Austen
uses in *Emma* when the heroine suspects that the illegitimate

---

[1] *The Female Quixote*, a new edition (London, 1820), Book I, chapter I.
[2] *Ibid.*

Harriet Smith is really a superior person who should marry someone better than a farmer; Harriet Smith, however, is no Perdita, and she marries her farmer in the end, not a Florizel. Arabella writes a note to her lover, which Lucy, her maid, re-writes, thus comically reversing the normal relationship. Emma has to correct the letter that Harriet writes, but its illiteracy does not disillusion her about the nobility of Harriet's character. There is a pretty milk-maid in *The Female Quixote* called Dolly Acorn, who resembles Harriet Smith. Though she says that she is daughter to a farmer, Arabella suggests that

in all probability, she was of a much higher extraction, if the picture you have drawn of her be true. The fair Arsinoe, princess of Armenia, was constrained for a while to conceal her true name and quality, and pass for a simple country-woman, under the name of Delia: yet the generous Philadelph, prince of Cilicia, who saw and loved her under that disguise, treated her with all the respect he would have done, had he known she was the daughter of a king.[1]

The conventional type of conduct book for young ladies, influenced by Richardson's novels, stressed the importance of obedience to parents, especially in their choice of husbands. The romantic attitude, burlesqued in *The Female Quixote*, involves an exaggerated vindication of the rights of woman, and a rejection of all restraint:

The impropriety of receiving a lover of her father's recommending appeared in its strongest light. What lady in romance ever married the man that was chosen for her? In those cases, the remonstrances of a parent are called persecutions; obstinate resistance, constancy and courage; and an aptitude to dislike the person proposed to them, a noble freedom of mind which disdains to love or hate by the caprice of others.[2]

This inversion of the conventional attitude is frequently adopted in Jane Austen's juvenilia, particularly *Love and Freindship*, but the romantic revolt against convention and even against ordinary sense also occurs in the mature novels. The sensibility of Marianne involves an unbalanced romanticism,

[1] *The Female Quixote*, Book VI, chapter 1.　　[2] *Ibid.* Book I, chapter 8.

akin to that of Arabella. Lydia Bennet's triviality is shown in a vulgar travesty of the romantic code, which provided a general excuse for the naughty girls of Jane Austen's novels.

Jane Austen made use of the conventions of romance both for serious and burlesque purposes. When writing in the burlesque mode, as in *Northanger Abbey*, it is her greater sensitiveness and control, her limited use of burlesque, which distinguish her work from that of Fielding and Mrs Lennox. The return to the normal world in *Northanger Abbey* is achieved naturally, because it has only been partly left.

At the end of *The Female Quixote* Mrs Lennox got help from Dr Johnson at the point in the story where a divine convinces the heroine that she has been acting foolishly. As a result, *The Female Quixote* ends in a completely arbitrary fashion. The heroine of *Northanger Abbey* is gradually brought back to normal by her own common sense, prompted by the enlightening hints of the hero. Despite the greater delicacy of her satire, however, Jane Austen retained her interest in burlesque even when she had out-grown this mode herself. She wrote to Cassandra in 1814 saying how amused and diverted she had been by *The Heroine, or adventures of a Fair Romance Reader*: 'a delightful burlesque, particularly on the Radcliffe style.'[1] The satire by E. S. Barrett is rather crude, even compared with that of Mrs Lennox, though it has exuberance and verve. No doubt, it stimulated Jane Austen in the revision of *Northanger Abbey*, originally written during 1797–8, and published posthumously in 1818. It shows the effect of an indiscriminate taste for sensation and sentiment, and exposes the false ideals of feminine behaviour inculcated in the novels that catered for this taste. It is strange that there should not have been a burlesque of the cult of the hero,[2] though Jane Austen attacks the falsely romantic, masculine type of character, such as Willoughby and Wickham, and ridicules sentimentality in men in the juvenilia.

[1] *Jane Austen's Letters*, ed. R. W. Chapman, p. 377.
[2] Fielding had burlesqued the 'rogue-hero' in *Jonathan Wild*, but there had been no similar deflation of the middle class ideal of 'the gentleman-hero' comparable to Molière's *Le Bourgeois Gentilhomme*.

She accepted the traditional, conventional ideas as to what made a gentleman or hero. She was much less satisfied about contemporary and traditional conceptions of the heroine or lady.

However, Jane Austen showed her usual critical shrewdness in using the conventions of the novel as written by Fanny Burney, who admired Dr Johnson, as a framework for her own fiction. *Evelina, Cecilia* and *Camilla*, despite their absurdities and limitations, which Jane Austen keenly appreciated, established a tradition for the woman novelist to follow. Of *Cecilia* it was recorded that 'it has drawn iron tears down cheeks that were never wetted with pity before; it has made novel readers of callous old maiden ladies, who have not for years received pleasure from anything but scandal'.[1] The greater refinement and subtlety of the later novelist is apparent in the greater range, flexibility and complexity of her style. Fanny Burney is notorious for her stilted Johnsonese, while Jane Austen usually avoids his mannerisms, though deeply influenced by him. Appreciating his wit as well as his moral seriousness, Jane Austen combines them, as he did, and the wisdom that emerges is sane and balanced. Imitating Dr Johnson more closely, Fanny Burney retains less of his essential spirit. There is a monotonous regularity in her style. Evelina writes in exactly the same weighted manner as her elders, and her difficulty in giving an accurate description of Captain Mirvan's nautical language is obviously shared by the author. This is a case of prudery, not necessarily of ignorance, for Fanny's brother James, who was to become an Admiral, went to sea at the age of ten.[2] Yet Evelina complains of Captain Mirvan that 'almost every other word he utters is accompanied by an oath...and besides he makes use of a thousand sea-terms, which are to me unintelligible'.[3] Such language would not have been strange to Jane Austen, whose admiration for the navy was also founded on knowledge. She must have been well acquainted with sea-

---

[1] G. E. Mitton, *Jane Austen and Her Times* (London, 1905), p. 56 (Mr Twining, writing to Dr Burney).

[2] See Joyce Hemlow, *The History of Fanny Burney* (Oxford, 1958), p. 9.

[3] *Evelina*, ed. Sir Frank D. Mackinnon (Oxford, 1930), vol. II, Letter 2.

terms, and if she had wished to introduce them into her novels could have supplemented her knowledge with that of her sailor brothers. In actual fact, the surly, vulgar and disagreeable sailor, Captain Mirvan, resembles the father of Fanny Price who embarrasses the heroine while she is staying in his sordid house in Portsmouth.

Fanny Burney and Jane Austen were both influenced by Fielding as well as by Dr Johnson. Again, Fanny Burney is more directly imitative, as, for example, in the scene where Evelina gets lost, and seeks protection from two women of low character, in whose company she is found by Lord Orville. The treatment of vulgar characters by Fanny Burney often gave Jane Austen a hint, and sometimes there is a common source in Fielding. In *Evelina* there is perpetual wrangling between Captain Mirvan and Madame Duval, who is also low-bred and 'illiberal'. Madame Duval is the model for Mrs Jennings in *Sense and Sensibility* and Mrs Bennet in *Pride and Prejudice*, characters which contrast in a similar way with the delicacy of the heroines. In *Emma*, when Mrs Elton remarks insincerely, 'I am doatingly fond of music—passionately fond',[1] she repeats the false exaggeration of Madame Duval who observed that 'music is my passion'.[2]

Occasionally, a solemn, pompous reflection of Fanny Burney is parodied. Thus, the moral Mr Villars writes to Evelina, 'Remember, my dear Evelina, nothing is so delicate as the reputation of a woman: it is, at once, the most beautiful and most brittle of all human things'.[3] When the serious Mary Bennet moralizes on the scandalous behaviour of her sister Lydia, she whispers to Elizabeth

This is a most unfortunate affair; and will probably be much talked of. But we must stem the tide of malice, and pour into the wounded bosoms of each other, the balm of sisterly consolation....Unhappy as the event must be for Lydia, we may draw from it this useful lesson; that loss of virtue in a female is irretrievable—that one false

---

[1] *Emma*, chapter 32. [2] *Evelina*, vol. i, Letter 23.
[3] *Ibid.* vol. ii, Letter 18.

step involves her in endless ruin—that her reputation is no less brittle than it is beautiful,—and that she cannot be too much guarded in her behaviour towards the undeserving of the other sex.[1]

Jane Austen accepts Fanny Burney's conception of the hero, but her heroines are much less conventional. Evelina blushes, a frequent habit of Fanny Burney's heroines, especially when the hero is present. The rudimentary psychology of her reactions and behaviour is limited to the portrayal of the struggle between reason, on the one hand, and imagination, fancy and passion on the other. 'Innocent as an angel, and artless as purity itself', she is supposed to have 'an excellent understanding and great quickness of parts', but we have to take these on trust. Her inexperience is, partly, that of Fanny Burney herself, exaggerated and dramatized. The author is similarly involved in the vulgarity of the Branghtons in *Evelina*, in a way that Jane Austen never is with her vulgar characters. Fanny Burney is too close to some of her characters and fascinated by others, as Richardson is with his creations. Evelina has some of Pamela's affected and doubtful ingenuousness, indulges in stilted Johnsonese even during her seduction, when it is most inappropriate, and is occasionally 'drowned' in tears of sensibility. Such a character was of less use to Jane Austen than the coarse Branghtons. Their self-confident folly, pretentiousness and sordidness inspired the satirical portrayal of the Steele sisters in *Sense and Sensibility*, being superimposed, in the case of Lucy, on the primary influence of Richardson's Pamela. In the same way they combine with Captain Mirvan to provide the model for the tone and atmosphere of the Portsmouth scenes in *Mansfield Park*.

The gentleman, as Fanny Burney describes him, derives from Richardson's Sir Charles Grandison. Air, address, 'countenance', person, manners, conversation and morals create the first favourable impression. Rank gives Lord Orville

---

[1] *Pride and Prejudice*, chapter 47. This parallel has been pointed out by R. Brimley Johnson, *The Women Novelists* (London, 1918), pp. 124–5. The whole chapter on parallel passages is interesting, though incomplete.

superiority; that he ignores his rank proves that his manners and understanding are such as to make him worthy of approval. The aristocratic hero who is gentle and unassuming, gifted but without bourgeois complacency, transcends, in an almost magical way, social barriers. 'O how different was his address! how superior did he look and move, to all about him!',[1] Evelina writes. This is the impression that Darcy first creates: 'Mr Hurst merely looked the gentleman; but his' (Mr Bingley's) 'friend soon drew the attention of the room by his fine, tall person, handsome features, noble mien; and the report which was in general circulation within five minutes after his entrance, of his having ten thousand a year.'[2] Jane Austen, realistically and shrewdly, deflates the glamorous heroic ideal, though she restores it later in the novel, and it reappears in the description of Mr Knightley at the ball at the Crown, 'so young as he looked! ...His tall, firm, upright figure, among the bulky forms and stooping shoulders of the elderly men, was such as Emma felt must draw every body's eyes...'.[3]

It was a unique compliment to take the phrase 'pride and prejudice' from the final summing-up of the moral of Fanny Burney's *Cecilia* and give it to what was probably, in certain respects, Jane Austen's own favourite novel.[4] Moreover, as Dr R. W. Chapman remarked, 'it is permissible to guess that "First Impressions"[5] owed more to *Cecilia* than the alteration of its title'.[6] A great number of parallel passages have been pointed out,[7] and the resemblances in character and plot noted:

Delvile, like Darcy, fell in love against his family instincts, and, with an equally offensive condescension, discoursed at length of his

---

[1] *Evelina*, vol. III, Letter 3.   [2] *Pride and Prejudice*, chapter 3.
[3] *Emma*, chapter 38.
[4] Recent correspondence in *The Times Literary Supplement*, 29 December 1961 and 26 January 1962, does not affect the primary claim of *Cecilia*, though in addition to the suggested alternatives, Gibbon and Jeremy Taylor, the phrase is also to be found in Cowper's *Hope*, l. 571, and Johnson's *The Idler*, no. 5.
[5] The first title by which *Pride and Prejudice* was known.
[6] See the appendix to *Pride and Prejudice* in Dr R. W. Chapman's edition, entitled '*Pride and Prejudice* and *Cecilia*'.
[7] See R. Brimley Johnson, *The Women Novelists*, pp. 117–30.

struggles between pride and passion to the young lady he desired to honour with his affection. He, too, resisted long, yielded in the end, and was forgiven. His mother's appeal to Cecilia was as violent and almost as impertinent, as Lady Catherine's to Elizabeth.[1]

Another critic goes so far as to say that 'the original conception of "First Impressions" was undoubtedly to re-write the story of "Cecilia" in realistic terms...and to contrast the romantic heroine's entry into the world ("Evelina") with the everyday equivalent'.[2]

Mortimer Delvile is an idealized character like Sir Charles Grandison and Lord Orville, when he is first introduced: he 'was tall and finely formed; his features, though not handsome, were full of expression; and a noble openness of manners and address spoke the elegance of his education, and the liberality of his mind'.[3] Fanny Burney is not able to show a character developing or changing or being transformed in the consciousness of another person (as Darcy's is in Elizabeth's); and her attitude to rank, and therefore to her hero, is humourlessly abject. When Cecilia is challenged by Mrs Delvile, whose family pride makes her oppose the marriage, her complete surrender contrasts with the defiance of Jane Austen's heroine. Her renunciation is based on a naïve acceptance of the convention of heroic perfection, as well as on a timid prostration in the face of social distinctions: 'Cecilia, scarce more afflicted than offended, now hastily answered, "Not for me, madam, shall he commit this crime, not on *my* account shall he be reprobated by his family! Think of him, therefore, no more with any reference to me, for I would not be the cause of unworthiness or guilt in him to be mistress of the universe!"'[4] At such crucial moments, Fanny Burney seems to foreshadow the schoolgirl's magazine rather than the mature and subtle art of Jane Austen.

Subjects of conversation in Fanny Burney's novels sometimes gave Jane Austen a hint. Thus, Mr Meadows in *Cecilia* expresses

[1] R. Brimley Johnson, *The Women Novelists*, p. 119.
[2] Q. D. Leavis, *Scrutiny*, vol. x, no. 1, p. 71.
[3] *Cecilia*, ed. A. R. Ellis (London, 1901), vol. i, book ii, chapter 6.
[4] *Ibid.* vol. ii, book vii, chapter 8.

his opinion of dancing: 'What, dancing? Oh, dreadful! how it was ever adopted in a civilised country, I cannot find out; it is certainly a Barbarian exercise, and of savage origin.'[1] In *Pride and Prejudice*, Sir William Lucas having remarked that dancing is one of the first refinements of polished society, Darcy retorts: 'It has the advantage also of being in vogue amongst the less polished society of the world.—Every savage can dance.'[2] This subject is discussed elsewhere in Jane Austen's novels. Darcy says that it is a subject which always makes a lady energetic; Mr Knightley considers that dancing, like virtue, must be its own reward; while Henry Tilney develops the idea that a country dance is an emblem of marriage.

Characters in *Cecilia* refer self-consciously to 'the TON' in a way that is no longer done by Jane Austen's young men and women. There are other examples of the manner in which Fanny Burney's portrayal of the social scene has become 'dated' by the second decade of the nineteenth century, though it is still possible for the later novelist to absorb the main outlines of the picture of society described in the fiction of her predecessor. Mr Gosport, in *Cecilia*, satirically indulges in some elementary psychology:

The TON misses, as they are called, who now infest the town, are in two divisions, the SUPERCILIOUS, and the VOLUBLE. The SUPERCILIOUS, like Miss Leeson, are silent, scornful, languid, and affected, and disdain all converse but with those of their own set; the VOLUBLE, like Miss Larolles, are flirting, communicative, restless, and familiar, and attack, without the smallest ceremony, every one they think worthy their notice. But this they have in common, that at home they think of nothing but dress, abroad, of nothing but admiration, and that everywhere they hold in supreme contempt all but themselves.[3]

One may compare the supercilious Miss Leeson and the voluble Miss Larolles with Jane Fairfax and Miss Bates in *Emma*, but Fanny Burney's social world is centred on London, while Jane Austen prefers the village and the small country-town. The

---

[1] *Ibid.* vol. I, book IV, chapter 7. [2] *Pride and Prejudice*, chapter 6.
[3] *Cecilia*, vol. I, book I, chapter 5.

social backgrounds of Jane Fairfax and Miss Bates are completely different from those of Miss Leeson and Miss Larolles. When Mr Gosport suggests three possible subjects of conversation—dress, public places and love—his satire has the type of general significance that Jane Austen's has for the reader of the twentieth century. When he remarks that 'a man of the *Ton*, who would now be conspicuous in the gay world, must invariably be insipid, negligent, and selfish',[1] one is aware both of the perennial nature of such a type and of the particular historical associations of Fanny Burney's example. Mr Meadows, whom Mr Gosport mentions as being at the head of the sect called 'the insensibilists', and Captain Aresby who belongs to the sect of 'the jargonists', represent a crude and clumsy attempt at the kind of social discrimination which Jane Austen presented through speech and dramatic action.

The skill of Jane Austen in transforming the material that Fanny Burney supplied is particularly apparent when there is a direct verbal reminiscence or use of an almost identical situation. In Fanny Burney's *Camilla*, to which Jane Austen subscribed, a lady called Eugenia says: 'Ah, my dear Uncle! how kind a memory is your's! retaining only what can give pleasure, and burying in oblivion whatever might cause pain!'[2] The stale cliché is omitted by Elizabeth Bennet when she consoles Darcy with the words 'You must learn some of my philosophy. Think only of the past as its remembrance gives you pleasure.'[3]

At one point in *Camilla*, the hero, Edgar Mandlebert, is handed some letters by the heroine, and his response described: 'Penetrated by this unexpected openness and compliance, he snatched her hand, with intent to press it to his lips; but again the recollection he had seen that liberty accorded to Sir Sedley, joined to the sight of his writing, checked him: he let it go; bowed his thanks with a look of grateful respect, and attempt-

---

[1] *Cecilia*, vol. I, book IV, chapter 2.
[2] *Camilla, or, A Picture of Youth* (London, 1796), book IV, chapter 9.
[3] *Pride and Prejudice*, chapter 52.

ing no more to stop her, walked towards the summer-house, to peruse the letters.'[1] This incident is used in *Emma* in the scene where the heroine meets Mr Knightley at Hartfield, after she has apologised to Miss Bates for her rudeness during the party at Box Hill. Mr Knightley is jealous of Frank Churchill, at this point in the story, just as Edgar Mandlebert is in *Camilla*, and his actions are almost the same, the result of a similar mingling of hope and fear:

He looked at her with a glow of regard. She was warmly gratified—and in another moment still more so, by a little movement of more than common friendliness on his part.—He took her hand—whether she had not herself made the first motion, she could not say—she might, perhaps, have rather offered it—but he took her hand, pressed it, and certainly was on the point of carrying it to his lips—when, from some fancy or other, he suddenly let it go. Why he should feel such a scruple, why he should change his mind when it was all but done, she could not perceive.—He would have judged better, she thought, if he had not stopped.—The intention, however, was indubitable; and whether it was that his manners had in general so little gallantry, or however else it happened, but she thought nothing became him more.—It was with him, of so simple yet dignified a nature.—She could not but recall the attempt with great satisfaction. It spoke such perfect amity.—He left them immediately afterwards—gone in a moment. He always moved with the alertness of a mind which could neither be undecided nor dilatory, but now he seemed more sudden than usual in his disappearance.[2]

Here one can see Jane Austen at work on the detail and texture of the prose of the original, developing an idea at one point, omitting or curtailing at another, just as she did when she revised the cancelled chapter of *Persuasion*. Mr Knightley, the perfect gentleman, 'takes' Emma's hand; Edgar Mandlebert 'snatches' Camilla's. Emma *thinks* that she made the first movement; there is no mention of Camilla doing so. Edgar snatches the hand 'with intent to press it to his lips'; Mr Knightley, more dignified and less impetuous, 'was on the point of carrying it to his lips'. Edgar lets the hand go; Mr Knightley 'suddenly' lets it go. Then Jane Austen describes in detail

---

[1] *Camilla*, book VII, chapter 9.   [2] *Emma*, chapter 45.

Emma's reactions to the situation and her new appraisal of the character of Mr Knightley, which is what really interests her. One notes how the very rhythms of Jane Austen's prose suggest the bold, decisive movements of her hero, and how the short sentences and staccato clauses convey Emma's flutterings, too: 'He left them immediately afterwards—gone in a moment. He always moved with the alertness of a mind which could neither be undecided nor dilatory, but now he seemed more sudden than usual in his disappearance.' Edgar's actions are comparatively conventional and unexciting, and Fanny Burney views the situation externally as just another incident in the story, which we do not share or take part in, as we do in *Emma*. The quality of the writing, particularly the use of rhythm, is what makes the scene between Emma and Mr Knightley so vivid.[1]

One of the most popular of the women novelists during the last fifteen years of the eighteenth century was Charlotte Smith, whose influence on Jane Austen has already been glanced at in connection with the use of picturesque and natural scenes as a background to the novels.[2] Charlotte Smith began her career as a novelist by translating *Manon Lescaut* (1785), a sign of comparative sophistication during a period when standards of taste in the novel were declining generally. Mary Lascelles has contrasted Charlotte Smith's Emmeline and Jane Austen's Catherine Morland.[3] Emmeline formed correct literary tastes in a ruined library and was mistress of every useful and ornamental feminine employment, without her receiving any instruction in them at all. Catherine 'never could learn or understand any thing before she was taught; and sometimes not even then, for she was often inattentive, and occasionally stupid'.[4] Whereas Emmeline 'was able to execute a faultless portrait of her Delamere (and leave it, wrapped in silver paper,

---

[1] Fanny Burney may have been influenced by Sterne who describes in *A Sentimental Journey* how he took a French lady's hand at Calais.

[2] See chapter 3, 'The Picturesque', pp. 50–1 above.

[3] Mary Lascelles, *Jane Austen and her Art*, p. 60.

[4] *Northanger Abbey*, chapter 1.

on the pianoforte, for him to discover there)',[1] Catherine 'had no notion of drawing—not enough even to attempt a sketch of her lover's profile, that she might be detected in the design'.[2] On the other hand, in *Mansfield Park*, Fanny Price goes to 'her nest of comforts', 'to see if by looking at Edmund's profile she could catch any of his counsel'.[3] Emmeline and Delamere discuss 'the *Sorrows of Werter*', whereas Jane Austen, in the early burlesque *Love and Freindship*, describes a character of whom it is said 'he was Sensible, well-informed, and Agreeable; we did not pretend to Judge of such trifles, but as we were convinced he had no soul, that he had never read the Sorrows of Werter, and that his Hair bore not the least resemblance to auburn, we were certain that Janetta could feel no affection for him, or at least that she ought to feel none'.[4] In *Northanger Abbey* Jane Austen ridicules the sentimental and romantic conventions of Charlotte Smith by contrasting with them an ordinary, simple girl taken from everyday life and described realistically. In *Love and Freindship*, sentimentality and romance are ridiculed by exaggerating them to absurd proportions. This is the method that is used in the later part of *Northanger Abbey*, when Jane Austen is satirizing the horror and terror story and its conventions.

Occasionally, Jane Austen may be indebted to Charlotte Smith for an odd phrase, or she may mock a certain cliché or vulgarism used by the less critical novelist. Thus, in *Ethelinde, or the Recluse of the Lake*, by Charlotte Smith, a character asks 'if Lord Danesforte is not the thing, who is?'[5] In *Emma*, Mr Woodhouse considers that Frank Churchill 'is not quite the thing'.[6] There are two characters called Selina and Emma in Charlotte Smith's *The Old Manor House*, whose names Jane Austen may have ironically taken for the heroine and the sister of the hated

---

[1] Mary Lascelles, *Jane Austen and her Art*, p. 60.
[2] *Northanger Abbey*, chapter 1.　　　[3] *Mansfield Park*, chapter 16.
[4] Jane Austen, *Minor Works*, p. 93.
[5] Charlotte Smith, *Ethelinde, or the Recluse of the Lake*, second edition (London, 1790), vol. II, p. 193.
[6] *Emma*, chapter 29.

Mrs Elton in her story. At one point in Charlotte Smith's novel, the heroine Isabella calls a General 'her old beau',[1] the very same familiar phrase used by the vulgar Mrs Elton to describe Mr Woodhouse. A few pages later in Charlotte Smith's novel, another vulgarism appears. Again it is the heroine who is guilty. She says 'Selina and Emma may determine to die old maids if they please; but, for my part, I'll try, as long as I am young and good looking, for a husband; and as to this Warwick, I am bent upon setting my cap at him without mercy, if his uncle would but give me an opportunity'.[2] In *Sense and Sensibility*, it is the vulgar Sir John Middleton, talking to Marianne and referring to Willoughby, who says 'You will be setting your cap at him now, and never think of poor Brandon'. To which Marianne replies indignantly, 'That is an expression, Sir John...which I particularly dislike. I abhor every common-place phrase by which wit is intended; and "setting one's cap at a man" or "making a conquest", are the most odious of all. Their tendency is gross and illiberal; and if their construction could ever be deemed clever, time has long ago destroyed all its ingenuity.'[3] Sir John does not understand this reproof. The coarseness, however, is not only his, but Charlotte Smith's whose lack of fastidiousness is being satirically reproached.

The genius of Shakespeare consists partly in the way in which he transcended the limitations of his stage and its conventions, turning what appear to be artificialities into a means of achieving the particular effects at which he was aiming. Similarly, Jane Austen turns inferior work by her predecessors and contemporaries to positive and constructive uses. However much she may satirize Charlotte Smith, one can still see a resemblance between the heroine of *The Old Manor House*, Isabella, and Jane Austen's Emma. The former is not exactly a coquette, but she has a greater flow of spirits than any of her family. She has a

---

[1] Charlotte Smith, *The Old Manor House*, ed. Mrs Barbauld (The British Novelists; vol. 36, London, 1810), vol. i, p. 183.

[2] *Ibid.* p. 187.

[3] *Sense and Sensibility*, chapter 9.

brother, who resembles Frank Churchill, and shows the same thoughtless vivacity as she does: 'from her sex and education, what was in him attended with dangerous errors, was in her only wild but innocent gaiety, becoming enough to youth, health and beauty. Of that beauty she had early learned the value: she had heard it praised at home, and found her father and mother were pleased to hear of it.'[1] On the other hand, Isabella goes to London, and in the experience of the rustic beauty in the metropolis, one is reminded of the experience of Elinor and Marianne, with the latter of whom Charlotte Smith's heroine has also some points in common. Isabella is admired by a General Tracy, a friend of her father, and of about his age. Her elderly admirer strikes the heroine as harmless though ridiculous, and the relationship between them foreshadows that between Marianne and Colonel Brandon. However, Charlotte Smith's main contribution to fiction was to the Gothic Romance: 'It is Charlotte Smith, herself a poet, who first begins to explore in fiction the possibilities of the Gothic castle, and her *Emmeline* (1788) is the first heroine whose beauty is seen glowing against that grim background, or who is hunted along the passages at night.'[2] As such, Charlotte Smith's fiction was only of negative use to Jane Austen in providing burlesque material for *Northanger Abbey*. The relationship with the greatest practitioner of the Gothic mode in English fiction, Ann Radcliffe, was more complicated, including a much greater degree of sympathy and identification.

In *Mansfield Park*, Fanny Price's favourite room has 'three transparencies, made in a rage for transparencies, for the three lower panes of one window, where Tintern Abbey held its station between a cave in Italy and a moonlight lake in Cumberland'.[3] The transparency representing 'a cave in Italy' may have been inspired by the novels of Ann Radcliffe. There are, in fact, a number of parallels between *The Mysteries of Udolpho*

[1] Charlotte Smith, *The Old Manor House* (The British Novelists), vol. 1, p. 182.
[2] J. M. S. Tompkins, *The Popular Novel in England, 1770–1800* (London, 1932), p. 266.
[3] *Mansfield Park*, chapter 16.

and *Mansfield Park*. Ann Radcliffe's novel opens in France with a description of the château of Monsieur St Aubert, 'on the pleasant banks of the Garonne'. It has a library, but the St Auberts live according to nature, for which they are enthusiasts, like Fanny Price. Emily's room appears to be the model for Fanny's:

Adjoining the eastern side of the greenhouse, looking towards the plains of Languedoc, was a room which Emily called hers, and which contained her books, her drawings, her musical instruments, with some favourite birds and plants. Here she usually exercised herself in elegant arts, cultivated only because they were congenial to her taste, and in which native genius, assisted by the instructions of Monsieur and Madame St Aubert, made her an early proficient. The windows of this room were particularly pleasant; they descended to the floor, and, opening upon a little lawn that surrounded the house, the eye was led between groves of almond, palm trees, flowering-ash, and myrtle, to the distant landscape, where the Garonne wandered.[1]

Fanny Price's nest is in the former school-room, and 'was quite deserted, except by Fanny, when she visited her plants, or wanted one of the books, which she was still glad to keep there, from the deficiency of space and accommodation in her little chamber above'.[2] 'The aspect' of the east room in *Mansfield Park* 'was so favourable, that even without a fire it was habitable in many an early spring, and late autumn morning.... Her plants, her books—of which she had been a collector, from the first hour of her commanding a shilling—her writing desk, and her works of charity and ingenuity, were all within her reach.'[3] There is, of course, an element of burlesque in Jane Austen's treatment of her heroine, which is lacking in Ann Radcliffe. Fanny Price, 'giving air to her geraniums', to see if by doing this 'she might inhale a breeze of mental strength herself', is more a self-conscious worshipper of nature than Emily, and represents an ironical comment on the ideas of Rousseau and Wordsworth which were so generally prevalent.

[1] Ann Radcliffe, *The Mysteries of Udolpho* (Everyman's Library edition), vol. I, p. 3.   [2] *Mansfield Park*, chapter 16.   [3] *Ibid.*

There is an 'improver', M. Quesnel, in *The Mysteries of Udolpho*, who suggests Mr Rushworth in *Mansfield Park*. M. Quesnel means to cut down some of the trees which encumber the château, and particularly offends St Aubert by threatening to destroy a noble chestnut.[1] Similarly Mr Rushworth suggests that the avenue at Sotherton should be cut down, whereupon Fanny quotes Cowper.[2]

The influence of Shakespeare on Ann Radcliffe has been frequently noted, and he is cited at the beginning of some of the chapters in *The Mysteries of Udolpho*. In *Mansfield Park*, Jane Austen occasionally appears to have absorbed Shakespeare through the medium of Ann Radcliffe. Thus, there is a typically romantic description in *The Mysteries of Udolpho* of the small and ancient town of Susa, which had formerly guarded the pass of the Alps into Piedmont. The romantic heights are seen by moonlight,

and here Emily first caught a strain of Italian music on Italian ground. As she sat, after supper, at a little window that opened upon the country, observing an effect of the moonlight on the broken surface of the mountains, and remembering that on such a night as this she once had sat with her father and Valancourt resting upon a cliff of the Pyrenees, she heard from below the long-drawn notes of a violin, of such tone and delicacy of expression as harmonized exactly with the tender emotions she was indulging, and both charmed and surprised her.[3]

When a comparable scene occurs in *Mansfield Park*, Jane Austen's sympathy with the heroine is modified by irony. 'When I look out on such a night as this', Fanny Price remarks, 'I feel that there could be neither wickedness nor sorrow in the world; and there certainly would be less of both if the sublimity of nature were more attended to, and people were carried more out of themselves by contemplating such a scene.'[4] Fanny Price recalls the same speech in *The Merchant of Venice*, Act v,

---

[1] *The Mysteries of Udolpho*, vol. I, p. 13.

[2] *Mansfield Park*, chapter 6. For the relationship of this passage to Gilpin, see chapter 3, 'The Picturesque', p. 56.

[3] *The Mysteries of Udolpho*, vol. I, p. 172.

[4] *Mansfield Park*, chapter 11.

scene 1, that Emily had remembered.[1] Jane Austen here has also been influenced by Wordsworth.[2]

Later in *The Mysteries of Udolpho*, Emily returns to Gascony and the Garonne, and is overcome by emotion at the sight of 'this beloved landscape', with the memories of Valancourt,

interesting and benevolent, as he had been wont to appear in the days of their early love...'Ah!' said Emily as she ascended, 'these are the same high trees that used to wave over the terrace, and these the same flowery thickets—the laburnum, the wild rose, and the cerinthe—which were wont to grow beneath them! Ah! and there too, on that bank are the very plants which Valancourt so carefully reared!—Oh, when last I saw them!'—She checked the thought, but could not restrain her tears; and after walking slowly on for a few minutes, her agitation upon the view of this well-known scene increased so much, that she was obliged to stop, and lean upon the wall of the terrace. It was a mild and beautiful evening. The sun was setting over the extensive landscape, to which his beams, sloping from beneath a dark cloud that overhung the west, gave rich and partial colouring, and touched the tufted summits of the groves that rose from the garden below with a yellow gleam.[3]

In *Mansfield Park*, it was 'a beautiful evening, mild and still', when Fanny Price and the rest of the party drove back from Sotherton.[4] Wordsworth had written 'It is a beauteous evening calm and free', when he composed his sonnet on the beach of Calais. Did Wordsworth remember *The Mysteries of Udolpho*, or did his sister remind him of it? Did Jane Austen recall Wordsworth's sonnet, or is the passage in *Mansfield Park* a direct reminiscence of *The Mysteries of Udolpho*? There can be little doubt that Jane Austen had the passage from Ann Radcliffe's novel in mind, but it seems that no definite answer can be given to the other questions.

The relationship of Jane Austen to her predecessors is not always so clear as it is in the cases of Fanny Burney, Charlotte Smith, and Ann Radcliffe. Often one has to rely on hints and

[1] See chapter 4, 'Drama and Poetry', pp. 70–2 above for Shakespearian influence generally on *Mansfield Park*. See also p. 78 above.
[2] See p. 78 above.   [3] *The Mysteries of Udolpho*, vol. II, pp. 253–5.
[4] *Mansfield Park*, chapter 10.

suggestions which the first readers of the novels would have detected far more easily. For example, it is known that Jane Austen made use of Mrs Inchbald's translation, *Lovers' Vows*, of a play by Kotzebue, the one which was acted at Mansfield Park. When, in *Emma*, Mr Knightley refers to the reconciliation between Harriet and Mr Martin, he says 'it is a very simple story'.[1] *A Simple Story*, published in 1791, was the more popular of Mrs Inchbald's novels, and one of the best-sellers of the age, admired by lady novelists and readers from Maria Edgeworth to Charlotte Brontë. The heroine of the first part of Mrs Inchbald's *A Simple Story* is a Miss Milner, unstable like Harriet Smith but also intelligent like Emma herself. May not Mr Knightley be slyly suggesting this comparison to Emma?

Mrs Inchbald approaches Jane Austen most closely in the sureness and delicacy of her irony and style. The story is confined to the relations of a few individuals, and 'the most poignant scene...takes place upon a stair-case which has never been described'.[2] It has been argued that the influences behind the book are French rather than English: 'It is among the followers of the French classical tradition that she must be placed. *A Simple Story* is, in its small way, a descendant of the tragedies of Racine, and Miss Milner may claim relationship with Madame de Clèves.'[3]

The novel is divided into two parts, the second of which is inferior, though it influenced Charlotte Brontë's *Jane Eyre*. The heroine of the first part, Miss Milner, is described by one of the other characters who disliked her, as 'young, idle, indiscreet, and giddy, with half-a-dozen lovers in her suite'.[4] To her admirers, she has 'beauty, united with sense and virtue'. Yet she is not perfect, as the heroines of Richardson and Fanny Burney had tended to be:

From her infancy she had been indulged in all her wishes to the extreme of folly, and started habitually at the unpleasant voice of

[1] *Emma*, chapter 54.
[2] Elizabeth Inchbald, *A Simple Story*, ed. G. L. Strachey (London, 1908), Introduction, p. iv.   [3] *Ibid.*   [4] *Ibid.* p. 11.

control. She was beautiful; she had been too frequently told the high value of that beauty, and thought every moment passed in wasteful idleness during which she was not gaining some new conquest. She had a quick sensibility, which too frequently discovered itself in the immediate resentment of injuries or neglect. She had, besides, acquired the dangerous character of wit; but to which she had no real pretensions, although the most discerning critic, hearing her converse, might fall into this mistake. Her replies had all the effect of repartee, not because she possessed those qualities which can properly be called wit, but that what she said was delivered with an energy, an instantaneous and powerful conception of the sentiment, joined with a real or well-counterfeited simplicity, a quick turn of the eye, and an arch smile. Her words were but the words of others, put into common sentences; but the delivery made them pass for wit, as grace in an ill-proportioned figure will often make it pass for symmetry.[1]

Miss Milner bears many resemblances to Isabella, the heroine of Charlotte Smith's *The Old Manor House*,[2] and to Jane Austen's Emma. All three heroines reflect changes in ideas on woman's rôle in society, and the contrast with Fanny Burney is extreme. Fanny Burney was a natural conservative in these matters and the older code survived even in her later novels. Her heroines, modelled on those of Richardson, are more or less passive embodiments of virtue, easy victims who needed the protection of their parents, and in their absence, had to be rescued by the hero. Just as Fanny Burney imitated Dr Johnson in a direct and obvious way, she had made use of some of the many books of courtesy,[3] which rivalled the novel itself in popularity with the general public.

For Fanny Burney, prudence, decorum and modesty were the virtues most necessary in a heroine, and with these virtues an acceptance of masculine superiority. Miss Milner, Isabella and Emma, on the other hand, partly resemble Congreve's Millamant and Shakespeare's heroines in their wit, and, without being blue-stockings or self-conscious feminists, have some of

---

[1] *A Simple Story*, p. 15.   [2] See pp. 104–5 above.
[3] See Joyce Hemlow, 'Fanny Burney and the Courtesy Books', *P.M.L.A.* vol. LXV, p. 734.

the confidence and independence of 'the new woman'. Miss Milner thought that 'as a woman, she was privileged to say anything she pleased; and, as a beautiful woman, she had a right to expect that whatever she pleased to say, should be admired'.[1] This is Emma's attitude, too.

When Dorriforth, the hero of *A Simple Story*, becomes Lord Elmwood, 'the acquisition of a title and an estate was, in Miss Milner's eye, an inestimable advantage to her guardian', though it does not alter her opinion of him as a person. Similarly, both Elizabeth Bennet and Emma approve of their husbands' wealth, but this approval does not in any way prevent them from making an impartial judgement of their conduct and behaviour. Such an attitude is very different from that of the conventional Pamelas of fiction, or even from that of the Evelinas. In Jane Austen, a sensible attitude towards rank is accompanied by a realistic, unsentimental but compassionate attitude towards poverty. When Emma visits the poor, 'she understood their ways, could allow for their ignorance and their temptations, had no romantic expectations of extraordinary virtue from those for whom education had done so little'.[2]

In *A Simple Story*, Mrs Inchbald refers to 'the unmeaning language of the world'. Both she and Jane Austen detect and expose the evil in the apparently good character, and the good in the apparently uninteresting. Dorriforth is no more a model of perfection than the heroine: 'Although Dorriforth was the good man that he has been described, there were in his nature shades of evil—there was an obstinacy which he himself and his friends termed firmness of mind; but had not religion and some opposite virtues weighed heavily in the balance, it would frequently have degenerated into implacable stubbornness.'[3] Dorriforth, regarded critically, with the quality of obstinacy particularly stressed, resembles Darcy, and viewed favourably reminds one of Mr Knightley.

---

[1] *A Simple Story*, p. 36.   [2] *Emma*, chapter 10.
[3] *A Simple Story*, p. 31.

The difference between Mrs Inchbald and Jane Austen on the one hand, and Fanny Burney on the other, is, in part, in the very quality of the writing which communicates their more sensitive and subtle insights. They concentrate pages of direct comments on morals and manners into a brief and revealing implicit criticism. Acutely aware of the nuances and implications of conversation, their dialogue is sufficiently flexible to record them. Thus, in *A Simple Story*, two characters pass judgement on the heroine, and, in doing so, reveal their own characters. The author comments, 'How unimportant, how weak, how ineffectual are words in conversation—looks and manners alone express—for Miss Woodley with her charitable face and mild accents, saying she would not forgive, implied only forgiveness—while Mrs Horton, with her enraged voice and aspect, begging heaven to pardon the offender, palpably said, she thought her unworthy of pardon.'[1] There is a great refinement of the crude psychology of the earlier novelist, a much deeper insight into the emotional springs of human behaviour, accompanied by a profounder interest in the themes of hypocrisy and self-deception. The concern is not so much to show virtue triumphant as to show what a complicated thing virtue is. The heroines of Mrs Inchbald and Jane Austen are subjected to disillusionment and enlightenment about themselves and others, an education in candour. They are trained by experience to be honest about their feelings. Emotional sincerity is supplemented by intellectual honesty on such questions as the importance of money and rank, the value of which is recognized, but not made into a criterion of moral worth.

Another novelist who influenced Jane Austen was Maria Edgeworth. Her novel *Belinda* is mentioned, together with Fanny Burney's *Cecilia* and *Camilla*, at the end of the fifth chapter of *Northanger Abbey*, where Jane Austen is defending the prestige and status of the novel against those who would try to belittle it. Each of these stories is cited as a 'work in which

---

[1] *A Simple Story*, p. 17.

the greatest powers of the mind are displayed, in which the most thorough knowledge of human nature, the happiest delineation of its varieties, the liveliest effusions of wit and humour are conveyed to the world in the best chosen language. Now, had the same young lady been engaged with a volume of the *Spectator*. . . .' Yet Jane Austen is also referring to Maria Edgeworth when she mentions reproachfully

that ungenerous and impolitic custom so common with novel writers, of degrading by their contemptuous censure the very performances, to the number of which they are themselves adding—joining with their greatest enemies in bestowing the harshest epithets on such works, and scarcely ever permitting them to be read by their own heroine, who, if she accidentally takes up a novel, is sure to turn over its insipid pages with disgust. Alas! if the heroine of one novel be not patronized by the heroine of another, from whom can she expect protection and regard?[1]

It was in the advertisement to *Belinda*, which appeared in 1801, that Maria Edgeworth made the statement that provoked this reproach by Jane Austen in *Northanger Abbey*.[2] Maria Edgeworth wrote,

Every author has a right to give what appellation he may think proper to his works. The public has also a right to accept or refuse the classification that is presented.

The following work is offered to the public as a *Moral Tale*—the author not wishing to acknowledge a Novel. Were all novels like those of Madame de Crousay, Mrs Inchbald, Miss Burney, or Dr Moore, she would adopt the name of novel with delight. But so much folly, error, and vice are disseminated in books classed under this denomination, that it is hoped the wish to assume another title will be attributed to feelings that are laudable and not fastidious.[3]

Despite Jane Austen's objection to Maria Edgeworth's attack on the novel, and her spirited defence, her own stories are moral tales in the sense that Maria Edgeworth uses the term, and in a manner practised by Crabbe, whose poems *The*

[1] *Northanger Abbey*, chapter 5.
[2] This was first pointed out by C. Linklater Thomson, in *Jane Austen: A Survey* (London, 1929), pp. 45–6.
[3] Maria Edgeworth, *Belinda* (1801), 'The Advertisement'.

Borough and *Tales* were published in 1810 and 1812. Jane Austen's artistic problem was always that of reconciling the moral intention which lay behind her fiction, her natural comic instinct, and the taste of the public for which she wrote. In *Northanger Abbey* and *Sense and Sensibility*, where Jane Austen seems to be writing with the object of both educating and pleasing the reading public, the moral intention and the nature of the comedy are comparatively direct and obvious.

Jane Austen appreciated the faults and limitations of the fiction of her contemporaries, and the defence of the novel at the end of the fifth chapter of *Northanger Abbey* is so extreme as to suggest that she is not altogether convinced by it herself, and is introducing an element of exaggeration and caricature to indicate a certain satirical and ironical reserve. Yet this awareness did not prevent her from ridiculing in the same novel a John Thorpe, who thought that 'novels are all so full of nonsense and stuff; there has not been a tolerably decent one since Tom Jones, except the Monk'.[1] John Thorpe is, of course, hopelessly ignorant and confused, and the moral about novels and reading is drawn by the hero, Henry Tilney: 'The person, be it gentleman or lady, who has not pleasure in a good novel, must be intolerably stupid. I have read all Mrs Radcliffe's works, and most of them with great pleasure.'[2] However, at the end of the novel, we witness the disillusion of Catherine with the view of life presented in *The Mysteries of Udolpho*. Jane Austen's own attitude towards her craft was complex and paradoxical, a mingling of admiration for the best work of her predecessors and of satirical amusement at the common level of contemporary achievement. Over thirty years before *Northanger Abbey* was published, Clara Reeve had been forced to recognize the inferior status of the novel, and compared it unfavourably with other forms of literature. 'Who are they that read Novels?' she asks, 'not men of learning, for they despise them, not men of business, for they have other employments, not the rich and the great, for they have other

---

[1] *Northanger Abbey*, chapter 7.   [2] *Ibid.* chapter 14.

amusements. The middling rank of people then are the chief if not the only readers, but particularly the young, the volatile, the hearts most susceptible of all kinds of impressions.'[1]

In one of Jane Austen's letters to her sister Cassandra, she refers to another novel of Maria Edgeworth, when she comments on 'one of my vanities, like your not reading *Patronage*'.[2] In another letter, she ironically expresses her admiration by saying 'I have made up my mind to like no Novels really, but Miss Edgeworth's, Yours & my own'.[3] *Patronage* was published in 1814, too late to influence *Mansfield Park*, while Jane Austen was working on *Emma*. At one point in Maria Edgeworth's novel, there is an interesting, though slightly crude discussion of the Bath marriage-market.[4] Here one can see how the materialistic, and even mercenary attitude to marriage, of which Jane Austen has been accused, was generally accepted. A Mrs Chatterton is described, 'who has been leading her three *gawky* graces about from one watering place to another these six years, fishing and hunting, and hawking for husbands'.[5] The places to which the girls were taken were Bath, London, Tunbridge, Weymouth, and Cheltenham. The correct technique apparently, was first to take the eligible girl or girls to one of the spas or watering places previous to her 'London campaign'. There reports were spread concerning her accomplishments and social connections. To dispose of one's daughters to the best advantage, as it was called, to make a fashionable marriage, it was necessary to follow this procedure. A character called Mrs Percy, in *Patronage*, maintains that happy marriages can only be made where people have leisure, and opportunities of becoming really and intimately acquainted with each other's dispositions, but the fashionable Lady Jane considers that this involves burying one's daughters in the country, for life. Lady Jane says that she could not bear the thought of Mrs Percy's pretty Caroline 'blushing unseen', to which Mr Percy replies

[1] Clara Reeve, *The Progress of Romance* (Colchester, 1785), pp. 92–3.
[2] *Jane Austen's Letters*, ed. R. W. Chapman, p. 398.
[3] *Ibid.* p. 405.
[4] *Patronage* (London, 1814), vol. I, chapter 14.   [5] *Ibid.*

that they could not bear the thought of her ceasing to blush from being too much seen.

The Percys personify the point of view of 'sense'. They have no wish to fit their daughters out and send them to the London market, to become the prey of the portionless class of matrimonial adventurers. The alternative, as they see it, is to keep their daughters in the bosoms of their own families, 'without seeking to entice or entrap, they can at all events never be disappointed, or degraded, and, whether married or single, will be respected and respectable, in youth and age; secure of friends, and of a happy home'.[1] Such a point of view, if taken to extremes, leads to the kind of opposition to marriage that is characteristic of Mr Woodhouse in Jane Austen's *Emma*. But it is also the attitude of Emma and Mr Knightley themselves, who consider that Hartfield and Highbury, within easy reach of London, represent a self-sufficient social unit, within which one can live satisfactorily. The danger of this point of view is that it tends to ignore the person of outstanding intelligence, character or beauty. It is only when there seems to be a possibility that Mr Knightley will marry Harriet Smith, that Emma appreciates this danger:

Could it be?—No; it was impossible. And yet it was far, very far, from impossible.—Was it a new circumstance for a man of first-rate abilities to be captivated by very inferior powers? Was it new for one, perhaps too busy to seek, to be the prize of a girl who would seek him? Was it new for anything in this world to be unequal, inconsistent, incongruous—or for chance and circumstance (as second causes) to direct the human fate?[2]

Later in the discussion in *Patronage*, Lady Jane observes that 'pretty well married' implies £2000 a year, and 'very well married', nothing under £10,000. This is the language of the market, to which Mr Percy replies that he is much more concerned with finding a man of sense, temper and virtue, who would love his daughter as she deserves to be loved. Jane Austen's Mr Knightley is just such a figure, and the marriage

[1] *Patronage*, vol. i, chapter 14.   [2] *Emma*, chapter 47.

which concludes the novel is a simple, unpretentious rustic affair, despised and ridiculed by the parvenue Mrs Elton. Yet, Mr Knightley is the wealthy owner of Donwell Abbey, and Emma has £30,000. Their marriage seems to represent the perfect combination of love, supported by material goods. In *Patronage*, Lady Jane refers to 'the saffron robe of Hymen' like Mrs Elton, but in each case the use of the sentimental cliché disguises the blatant materialism of their motives.

Maria Edgeworth is aware that ideas about marriage and other problems are not confined to the alternatives represented by provincial rural society and the metropolis. She introduces into *Patronage* two characters personifying an ideal superior to that of both the Percys and Lady Jane. They are Mrs Hungerford and her daughter Mrs Mortimer. The wife of Admiral Mortimer had passed some years abroad in her early youth, and is described as having the vivacity, ease, polish, tact and *esprit de société* of a Frenchwoman, with the solidity of understanding amiable qualities, domestic tastes and virtues of an Englishwoman. She and her mother, Mrs Hungerford, enjoy society both in town and in the country. Mrs Mortimer's house in London was 'the resort of the best company in the best sense of the word'. Whereas an English *conversazione* set people against their will and their nature to talk wit or reduced them, against their pride and conscience, to worship idols, this company partook of the best English and French society, judiciously combined. With French manners, there were English morals, with French ease, gaiety and politeness, English sincerity, confidence, and 'safety'.

Similar comparisons and contrasts are made in Jane Austen's *Persuasion*. The manners of Mrs Croft, the wife of the Admiral who takes over Kellynch Hall, the residence of Sir Walter Elliot, are described as 'open, easy, and decided, like one who had no distrust of herself'.[1] While Admiral Croft's manners were not quite of the tone to suit Lady Russell, they delight Anne. 'His goodness of heart and simplicity of character were

---

[1] *Persuasion*, chapter 6.

irresistible.'[1] Later, the heroine Anne compares the manners of
Mr Elliot, the nephew and heir of Sir Walter, with those of
Captain Wentworth, the naval hero of Jane Austen's final,
completed novel. Mr Elliot, despite his surface attractiveness,
turns out to be cunning, selfish and treacherous. His manners,
if not his morals, are obviously intended to resemble those of
Sir Walter and his favourite daughter Elizabeth, 'whose
entrance seemed to give a general chill. Anne felt an instant
oppression, and, wherever she looked, saw symptoms of the
same. The comfort, the freedom, the gaiety of the room was
over, hushed into cold composure, determined silence, or
insipid talk, to meet the heartless elegance of her father and
sister.'[2] That Captain Wentworth, though flattered and courted
by Sir Walter and Elizabeth, should completely despise them
and the 'best society' which they represent, shows that Jane
Austen's idea of good company is as distant from Lady Jane's in
Patronage, as that of Maria Edgeworth herself. Though Captain
Wentworth and Admiral Croft cannot be said to represent
civilized society in the sense that Mrs Mortimer and Mrs
Hungerford do in *Patronage*, they embody an ideal with which
the heroine can identify herself.

In *Patronage*, as in *A Simple Story*, one is very close to the world
of Jane Austen's novels, though the style of Maria Edgeworth's
writing is without the French clarity and irony of Mrs Inchbald's, however much Maria Edgeworth may have admired
the French. Her prose is without wit and epigrammatic grace.
Yet she admired *A Simple Story*, and wrote to Mrs Inchbald
explaining the reasons for her admiration:

I hope you will not suspect me of the common author's practice of
returning praise for praise, when I tell you that I have just been
reading, for the third—I believe for the fourth time—the *Simple
Story*. Its effect upon my feelings was as powerful as at the first
reading; I never read any novel—I except none—I never read any
novel that affected me so strongly, or that so completely possessed
me with the belief in the real existence of all the people it represents.

---

[1] *Persuasion*, chapter 13.   [2] *Ibid.* chapter 22.

I never once recollected the author whilst I was reading it; never said or thought, 'that's a fine sentiment'—or 'that is well expressed' —or 'that is well invented.' I believed all to be real, and was affected as I should be by the real scenes if they had passed before my eyes.[1]

Maria Edgeworth is describing an impersonality of art that she was herself not able to achieve. The detachment of her realism which was admired and imitated by Turgenev was not an art that had undergone the chastening influence of French, or that was illuminated by French esprit, even though she visited France in the years 1802–3, and her novels were translated into French and German. *Ormond* (1817), which deals partly with French life, appeared too late to influence Jane Austen, and she does not appear to have been interested in the educational ideas of Maria Edgeworth and her father, with their Rousseau-istic tendencies.

---

[1] Quoted by S. R. Littlewood, *Elizabeth Inchbald and her Circle* (London, 1921), p. 123.

CHAPTER 7

OTHER INFLUENCES

Jane Austen does not seem to have been deeply influenced by the realism of Smollett, who was, generally, too coarse for her to use in fiction, and when ridiculing sentiment, she rarely burlesqued Sterne, Goldsmith or Mackenzie. The relationship between sense and sensibility in her novels was delicate and subtle, and though she ridiculed excessive sensibility, she never excluded it completely from her ideal characters.

On the other hand, she read and enjoyed a great deal of literature of little permanent interest, seeing in it potential material for parody and burlesque. The horror and terror novels mentioned in *Northanger Abbey*, Mrs Parsons's *The Castle of Wolfenbach* and *The Mysterious Warning*, Regina Maria Roche's *Clermont*, Peter Teuthold's *The Necromancer: or The Tale of the Black Forest*, Francis Lathom's *The Midnight Bell*, Eleanor Sleath's *The Orphan of the Rhine*, and Peter Will's *Horrid Mysteries*, are typical of the mass of third-rate fiction which might still provide material for burlesque.[1] Jane Austen's reaction to both the sentimental novel and the horror-terror story was that of Crabbe in *The Borough*.[2]

The influence of French literature is difficult to estimate, but it is probably greater than has usually been assumed. In 1786, Eliza de Feuillide arrived at Steventon 'bringing with her a command of the French language, knowledge of the French court, and a talent for theatricals'.[3] Dr R. W. Chapman has noted references to Arnaud Berquin's *L'Ami de l'Adolescence*, Mme de Staël's *Corinne* (in translation), Mme de Genlis's

---

[1] See Michael Sadleir, 'The Northanger Novels: A Footnote to Jane Austen', English Association Pamphlet, 1927, and introduction to *Northanger Abbey* in The World's Classics Series.

[2] *The Borough* (1810), Letter xx. The Poor of the Borough: Ellen Orford.

[3] R. W. Chapman, *Jane Austen: Facts and Problems* (Oxford, 1948), p. 32.

Adelaide and Theodore, *Alphonsine*, *Les Veillées du Château*, and Mme de Sévigné's *Lettres*. It is strange that there should be no reference to Rousseau, whom Jane Austen must surely have read. In *La Nouvelle Héloïse*, Julie writes to Claire about the death of La Chaillot: 'elle était plutôt ton amie que ta gouvernante; elle t'aimait tendrement, et m'aimait parce que tu m'aimes; elle ne nous inspira jamais que des principes de sagesse et d'honneur'.[1] One is reminded here of the relationship between Emma and Miss Taylor: 'Sixteen years had Miss Taylor been in Mr Woodhouse's family, less as a governess than as a friend'.[2] As the character of La Chaillot is developed and portrayed in the next letter, however, the resemblance is rather to Miss Bates than to Miss Taylor: 'Je conviens que la pauvre mie était babillarde, assez libre dans ses propos familiers, peu discrète avec de jeunes filles, et qu'elle aimait à parler de son vieux temps.' Then the character changes again, and recalls Miss Taylor's relationship to Emma: 'Aussi ne sont-ce pas tant les qualités de son esprit que je regrette, bien qu'elle en eût d'excellentes parmi de mauvaises; la perte que je pleure en elle, c'est son bon coeur, son parfait attachement, qui lui donnait à la fois pour moi la tendresse d'une mère et la confiance d'une soeur.'[3]

In *Persuasion*, there is a point in the story where the heroine, Anne Elliot, possibly reflects the sentiments of Rousseau's Julie. After recommending books to Captain Benwick, 'Anne could not but be amused at the idea of her coming to Lyme, to preach patience and resignation to a young man whom she had never seen before; nor could she help fearing, on more serious reflection, that, like many other great moralists and preachers, she had been eloquent on a point in which her own conduct would ill bear examination'.[4] Julie observes, 'Je me doute bien qu'à l'exemple de l'inséparable tu m'appelleras aussi la *prêcheuse*, et il est vrai que je ne fais pas mieux ce que je dis que les gens du métier'.[5]

---

[1] *Julie ou La Nouvelle Héloïse*, Première Partie, Lettre VI.
[2] *Emma*, chapter I.
[3] *Julie ou La Nouvelle Héloïse*, Première Partie, Lettre VII.
[4] *Persuasion*, chapter 11.
[5] *Julie ou La Nouvelle Héloïse*, Première Partie, Lettre XLIV.

Persuasion also contains what is probably a reference to one of the most famous passages in Voltaire's *Candide*. Sir Walter Elliot, expressing his disgust at Admiral Baldwin's lack of attention to his personal appearance, remarks of such characters 'it is a pity they are not knocked on the head at once'.[1] There is almost certainly a reference here to the classic comment in *Candide* (recalling the sentence passed on Admiral Byng), 'Dans ce pays-ci il est bon de tuer de temps en temps un amiral pour encourager les autres'.[2] Previously, Sir Walter Elliot had complained of Lord St Ives, 'whose father we all know to have been a country curate, without bread to eat', and who may have been suggested by Lord Nelson himself, whose life by Southey Jane Austen had read.[3] G. M. Trevelyan has stated that 'the naval officers were now the sons of gentlemen of modest means (Nelson was a poor parson's son), sent to sea as boys, and combining what was best in the "tarpaulin's" experience and training with the manner and thought of an educated man. Fanny's brother William, in *Mansfield Park*, and Captain Wentworth in *Persuasion* stand for all that was most attractive in the type.'[4] Through her two brothers who were in the navy, one of whom just missed the Trafalgar action, Jane Austen would be particularly knowledgeable about such matters. Admiral Croft, who takes over Sir Walter Elliot's residence, was 'rear admiral of the white. He was in the Trafalgar action'.[5] Sir Walter Elliot, with his Voltairean wit, and his snobbish imitation of Lord Chesterfield's code of manners, is completely opposed to the stoicism of Dr Johnson and the fortitude of Nelson and his 'band of brothers'.[6]

It is possible that the protagonist of the sketch *Lady Susan* derives from French fiction. There is no parallel elsewhere in the novels for the polished, cynical and ruthless Lady Susan,

[1] *Persuasion*, chapter 3.   [2] *Candide*, chapter 23.
[3] *Jane Austen's Letters*, ed. R. W. Chapman, p. 345.
[4] G. M. Trevelyan, *English Social History* (London, 1946), p. 499.
[5] *Persuasion*, chapter 3.
[6] Voltaire's *Candide* came out in the same year as Dr Johnson's *Rasselas*, an all-important influence on Jane Austen.

except Mary Crawford in *Mansfield Park*, who probably is modelled on her.[1] There is a similar, though even more ruthless character, La Marquise de Merteuil, in the scandalous but highly successful novel *Les Liaisons dangereuses* of Choderlos de Laclos. Eliza de Feuillide, who came to England in 1786, had married the Comte in 1781, and the novel by Choderlos de Laclos was published in 1782. Laclos shared with Jane Austen an admiration for the novels of Fanny Burney, and published in 1784 an extended article, summarizing and reviewing *Cecilia*, in three numbers of the *Mercure de France*.[2] Henry Crawford, in *Mansfield Park*, may be regarded as a milder, anglicized version of the heartless seducer Valmont in Laclos's novel, while Edmund Bertram and Fanny Price represent in a more than usually direct and rigid form Jane Austen's own moral standards by which she criticizes the characters who, in the words of Mr Knightley about Frank Churchill, 'may be very "aimable", have very good manners, and be very agreeable; but. . . can have no English delicacy towards the feelings of other people, nothing really amiable about them'.[3] Valmont personifies the duplicity of the code of Lord Chesterfield, applied ruthlessly in sexual relationships, and Jane Austen may be considered as reacting against the immorality of both Lord Chesterfield and Laclos, while using the novel as the source of her study in evil in *Lady Susan* and *Mansfield Park*. There is certainly a large number of French words and phrases in *Mansfield Park*, seventeen examples, as opposed to five in *Sense and Sensibility*, four in *Pride and Prejudice*, seven in *Emma*, and three in *Northanger Abbey*. The majority of the words and phrases are commonplace.

Apart from Eliza de Feuillide, Jane Austen was greatly influenced by certain friends, of whom Mrs Lefroy was the most important, while acquaintances and neighbours were a frequent source of satirical amusement, as were her own family. Jane Austen's nephew states that while she was at Steventon,

[1] This is Q. D. Leavis's theory. See *Scrutiny*, vol. x, nos. 2 and 3.
[2] See Choderlos de Laclos, *Œuvres Complètes*, la bibliothèque de la Pléiade, p. 884.   [3] *Emma*, chapter 18.

'amongst the most valuable neighbours of the Austens were Mr and Mrs Lefroy and their family. He was rector of the adjoining parish of Ashe; she was sister to Sir Egerton Brydges, to whom we are indebted for the earliest notice of Jane Austen that exists'.[1] The brother and sister formed a complete and utter contrast with each other. 'Mrs Lefroy was a remarkable person. Her rare endowments of goodness, talents, graceful person, and engaging manners, were sufficient to secure her a prominent place in any society into which she was thrown; while her enthusiastic eagerness of disposition rendered her especially attractive to a clever and lively girl. She was killed by a fall from her horse on Jane's birthday, Dec. 16, 1804.'[2] Four years afterwards, this incident provoked the novelist to write verses *To the Memory of Mrs Lefroy*, which are an expression of emotion unique in directness and intensity.

Sir Egerton Brydges, the brother of Mrs Lefroy, has been neglected by biographers and critics because of his apparently minor importance in Jane Austen's life and his insignificance as a writer. Yet the mere fact that he was unimportant and personally unattractive was likely to increase his fascination for a novelist who was herself supremely modest and who appreciated the negative value of a limited and flawed talent from whose mistakes she could cautiously learn to achieve perfection.

Sir Samuel Egerton Brydges, to give him his full title, was educated at Maidstone School, at the King's School, Canterbury, and at Queens' College, Cambridge.[3] The author of the account of his literary career has written describing how in 1786, after his marriage, he moved into the country and settled in Hampshire, close to his sister Ann.

Because of her intimacy with the Austen family (she was then Mrs George Lefroy, Jane Austen's beloved 'Madame Lefroy') he was able to rent from the Reverend George Austen the parsonage at Deane. Thus it happened that Egerton Brydges joined for a time

---

[1] J. E. Austen-Leigh, *Memoir of Jane Austen*, ed. R. W. Chapman, pp. 49–50.
[2] *Ibid.* pp. 56–7.
[3] These and some of the later details are taken from the article in *The Dictionary of National Biography* by Warwick Wroth.

the happy company of Austens and Lefroys. He took some part in their theatrical entertainments, contributing, in spite of the grievance he nursed against the public, an epilogue for Mrs Centilivre's *The Wonder: A Woman Keeps a Secret*, a play which was acted in December 1787, almost the last of those theatricals conducted by the Austens at Steventon. Although he gave little attention to Jane Austen, who was then a girl in her teens, he recalled many years later her fair appearance and lamented his failure to realize that she was an authoress. From intimations in her letters, on the other hand, it is evident that she gave little consideration to the disappointed young poet. Indeed he must have been a moody, unsociable creature with his wounded feelings and his preference for solitary study. Most of his time he read biography and heraldry, subjects in which his interest had been awakened at the Middle Temple.[1]

Sir Egerton Brydges never practised at the bar, and retired in 1792 to Denton Court, a seat which he had purchased near his birthplace in Kent. In 1785 he published a volume of poems, which went to a fourth edition by 1807. His novels, *Mary de Clifford* (1792) and *Arthur Fitz-Albini* (1798) were fairly popular, the latter reaching a third edition by 1810, and being printed by the Minerva Press. Brydges began in 1806 a new and augmented edition of Collins's *Peerage of England*, a work which was eventually published in 1812 in nine volumes. He was not created an English baronet until 1814. His *Autobiography* came out in 1834 and he describes there Mrs Lefroy, the Austens, and 'Jane Austen, the novelist': 'When I knew Jane Austen I never suspected that she was an authoress; but my eyes told me that she was fair and handsome, slight and elegant, but with cheeks a little too full. The last time I think that I saw her was at Ramsgate in 1803: perhaps she was then about twenty seven years old. Even then I did not know that she was addicted to literary composition.'[2]

In Jane Austen's letters, the name of Brydges appears in connection with his second novel, *Fitz-Albini*. Jane Austen

[1] Mary Katherine Woodworth, *The Literary Career of Sir Samuel Egerton Brydges* (Oxford, 1935), pp. 7–8.

[2] *The Autobiography, Times, Opinions and Contemporaries of Sir Egerton Brydges* (London, 1834), vol. II, chapter 3, p. 41.

writes on 25 November 1798 from Steventon to her sister Cassandra, who is staying at Godmersham Park, Kent, the county in which Sir Samuel had his country seat: 'We have got "Fitz-Albini"; my father has bought it against my private wishes, for it does not quite satisfy my feelings that we should purchase the only one of Egerton's works of which his family are ashamed.'[1] Jane Austen makes it clear that she has no great opinion of these works, but her remark to Cassandra suggests that she had almost certainly read the novel which preceded *Fitz-Albini*, entitled *Mary de Clifford*, and published in 1792.

In the preface to this novel, Sir Samuel refers contemptuously to 'the generality of readers' who consider writings of the romantic class 'high-flown (as they term them), while they commend and peruse with avidity tales descriptive of more ordinary and daily life, which they call natural, as if nothing was natural that was not vulgar, or at least familiar'. Jane Austen must have read these pages with amusement, for she was to attain her popularity by 'lowering' her ideas to the sympathies of ordinary minds. In fact, *Elinor and Marianne*, the first version of *Sense and Sensibility*, written 1795–8, was a direct refutation of the sensibility and false, sentimental romanticism of *Mary de Clifford*, assuming that it resembled in its general outlines the finished novel. In 1794 Jane Austen was probably in Kent, near Sir Egerton's country seat.

There can be no doubt that *Mary de Clifford* represents a 'spontaneous overflow of powerful feelings', for, as the author says,

I have written these sheets with a degree of rapidity, which the public would not think the better of me for telling them. I have not written for reputation; it has been an exquisite amusement to me, a delightful relaxation from drier studies, to commit to paper, as carelessly as they rose, some of the thoughts that were playing about my fancy. Whatever faults there may be therefore, I think there cannot be those of affectation. As to the Poetry with which this little volume is pretty thickly sown, I never studied it, but frequently

---

[1] *Jane Austen's Letters*, ed. R. W. Chapman, p. 32.

OTHER INFLUENCES

found it easier to express the ideas that were pressing on my mind in
verse, than in prose; and then having once written down the lines
that were intended to preserve my thoughts, I let them stand,
without ever thinking any more about them.[1]

The hero of the novel is an obviously flattering indulgence
in autobiography, while his sister generally resembles Jane
Austen's Marianne, though occasionally she suggests Mary
Bennet in her earnest solemnity, and Fanny Price in her
humble, passive subservience:

Mary, to all the sensibility and taste of her brother, yet softened by
her sex, had something still more romantic in her turn; and tender
and docile as she was, caught all the enthusiasm of his sentiments;
which, though they were ever floating in her mind and gaining fresh
force there, broke not out in her expressions; for she was a silent
listener, and rather assented by her countenance, which was all
intelligence, than by her lips.
. . . without mixing with the world, or even enjoying the familiarity of any female of her own age, of whom there happened to be
none that the family visited within a convenient distance. Her mind
and sentiments, therefore, naturally in the highest degree delicate,
were purity itself. No books but the most elegant and refined had
fallen in her way. The most polite moralists, and the best poets were
selected from the heterogeneous mass, that were kept constantly
locked up in the cases of the fine old library, and placed on the
shelves of her little dressing-room, by the hands of her brother. With
a mind thus formed and educated, she had completed her sixteenth
year with such a degree of enjoyment as human life has seldom
furnished. All the scenery around her was in unison with her feelings. . . .[2]

The villain, Sir Peter Lumm, is the son of a rich woollen
draper, who has bought a large estate nearby. Sir Peter proposes to Mary and is rejected in an exchange of words that
recalls the famous scene in *Pride and Prejudice*, though it is Mary
who is guilty of both pride and prejudice in Brydges's novel.
First Impressions, the first version of Jane Austen's novel, was
written between October 1796 and August 1797. It would be

[1] *Mary de Clifford*, 2nd edition (London, 1811), preface, p. vi.
[2] *Ibid.* pp. 4–5.

interesting to know if it contained the scene of Darcy's proposal, and if this was the same as in its final form in *Pride and Prejudice*. The scene in *Mary de Clifford* is melodramatic, banal and slightly vulgar: '"Oh, if you did but know,"—replied he (affecting a soft voice) "the pangs of my heart—Oh! suffer me to lay my fortune and my life at your feet!"—"Sir"—(cried she in a firmer tone) "do you mean to add fresh insults to those you have already given me by this unmeaning nonsense!"' There is some resemblance between this, however, and the parallel scene in *Pride and Prejudice*, where Elizabeth remarks caustically to Mr Darcy, 'I might as well enquire...why with so evident a design of offending and insulting me, you choose to tell me that you liked me against your will, against your reason, and even against your character'.[1]

There is a similarity, too, between the passage that immediately follows in *Mary de Clifford* and two passages in Jane Austen's famous scene of proposal. '"Nonsense, madam!"' Sir Peter Lumm says, '"I assure you, I was never more in earnest in my life!"—"Nor was I then, Sir," (added she) "than when I say that, had you a thousand times your fortune, and ten thousand times the qualities upon which you most pride yourself, I would sooner work for my daily bread than be your wife!"'[2]

Elizabeth's words to Mr Darcy are equally severe, but more pointed and urbane: 'You are mistaken, Mr Darcy, if you suppose that the mode of your declaration affected me in any other way, than as it spared me the concern which I might have felt in refusing you, had you behaved in a more gentleman-like manner'.[3] Shortly after this, her words become even more bitter:

From the very beginning, from the first moment I may almost say, of my acquaintance with you, your manners impressing me with the fullest belief of your arrogance, your conceit, and your selfish disdain of the feelings of others, were such as to form that ground-work

---

[1] *Pride and Prejudice*, chapter 34. [2] *Mary de Clifford*, p. 109.
[3] *Pride and Prejudice*, ibid.

of disapprobation, on which succeeding events have built so immoveable a dislike; and I had not known you a month before I felt that you were the last man in the world whom I could ever be prevailed on to marry.[1]

The moral drawn from the interview by Brydges's aristocratic heroine is the opposite of that pointed by the encounter between Elizabeth and Darcy. 'I have not, Sir,' says Mary, 'inherited the blood of the de Cliffords without long knowing, that there is more pride and insolence in one house of new-got wealth, than in all the ancient families of England together!'[2] What one notices here is not merely the difference of the theme from that of *Pride and Prejudice* (though it has a certain relevance to Mr Collins), but the contrast in the quality of the language itself. Whereas Jane Austen refined the sentiments and expression of Fanny Burney and her followers, Brydges seems to represent a pretentious and debased imitation. One recalls that he admired the novels of Mrs Charlotte Smith, which he found an exception to what he considered the generally low level of fiction. He described her novels as 'productions of a very superior nature',[3] which had given him an exquisite pleasure increased by the congeniality of her ideas. They were both poets, though of an inferior kind, and in both cases poetry was the outlet for a lack of intellectual and emotional coherence and discipline. Brydges's biographer considers that *Mary de Clifford* is a descendant of the Richardsonian novel, especially *Sir Charles Grandison*; but it obviously belongs among the sentimental romances that followed the vogue of Walpole's *Castle of Otranto* and Mrs Clara Reeve's *Old English Baron*. Its ancient mansions with their galleries of portraits, old libraries, painted glass, and grim towers are all conventions derived from contemporary fiction. Nor are the pale, ineffectual hero, and the delicate heroine delighting in rural solitude, less inspired by the Gothic novels. We look in vain, however, for the trappings of horror. The villain is allowed only gruff manners and revenge in a duel.[4]

---

[1] *Pride and Prejudice*, chapter 34. [2] *Mary de Clifford*, p. 111.
[3] *Ibid*. The Preface, pp. iii–iv.
[4] Mary Katherine Woodworth, *The Literary Career of Sir Samuel Egerton Brydges*, p. 40.

It was in 1788 that Brydges read *Emmeline, or the Orphan of the Castle*, the novel of Charlotte Smith's that appears to have most influenced him.

The heroines of *Mary de Clifford* and of *Pride and Prejudice* both weep after the interview with their suitors, but Elizabeth delays her outburst of tears until Darcy has left, while 'Sir Peter, sullen with affronted pride, seemed to feel his revenge gratified by her weeping, and coldly took his leave'.[1]

It is immediately following this incident that Brydges's heroine gets the bottom of her petticoats wet, together with her ankles, which reminds one again of a parallel scene in *Pride and Prejudice*. In *Mary de Clifford*, 'The dews fell fast; and the bottoms of her petticoats that swept the grass, seemed wet almost as if dipped in water, while her thin silk stockings but ill protected her most slender and beautiful ankles from the damp. A drizzling rain began to fall before she reached the house; and with difficulty did she find time to change her dress before she heard the summons to dinner'.[2] After Elizabeth parts from Catherine and Lydia in Meryton, she 'continued her walk alone, crossing field after field at a quick pace, jumping over stiles and springing over puddles with impatient activity, and finding herself at last within view of the house, with weary ankles, dirty stockings, and a face glowing with the warmth of exercise'.[3] When dinner is over at Netherfield, Elizabeth retires immediately, 'and Miss Bingley began abusing her as soon as she was out of the room. Her manners were pronounced to be very bad indeed, a mixture of pride and impertinence; she had no conversation, no stile, no taste, no beauty'.[4] This reminds one of Mary's remark to Sir Peter Lumm that 'there is more pride and insolence in one house of new-got wealth, than in all the ancient families of England together!'. It appears that Jane Austen is satirizing the snobbishness of Sir Samuel's heroine. Yet Mrs Hurst's comment on Elizabeth repeats the description in *Mary de Clifford*: 'She has nothing, in short, to recommend her, but

[1] *Mary de Clifford*, p. 111.
[2] *Ibid.* p. 112.
[3] *Pride and Prejudice*, chapter 7.
[4] *Ibid.* chapter 8.

being an excellent walker. I shall never forget her appearance this morning. She really looked almost wild....Yes, and her petticoat; I hope you saw her petticoat, six inches deep in mud, I am absolutely certain; and the gown which had been let down to hide it, not doing its office.'[1] Jane Austen uses the incident described in *Mary de Clifford*, but transforms it by a slight exaggeration, adding to it in a way that makes the final result seem fresh and original.

There are two further examples of a possible relationship between the novels. De Clifford, the brother of the heroine, has a friend Mr Fitzherbert, whom he had known abroad, and who may have suggested to Jane Austen Colonel Fitzwilliam, nephew of Lady Catherine de Bourgh: it is not only their names that are similar; each of them is a man of ancient family. The incident in *Mary de Clifford* where Sir Peter's steward, John Higgins, writes to Woodvile, the hero, informing him that there is a mortgage on his property, may have suggested to Jane Austen the possibility of satirical treatment and produced the famous entail which causes such trouble in *Pride and Prejudice*. Woodvile replies romantically to the threat of the villain by remarking that 'ill-got wealth may confer rank on the person, but cannot elevate the mind'.[2] Jane Austen takes a much more realistic attitude towards wealth, and her heroine even suggests that it was the sight of the hero's magnificent grounds that made her alter her opinion about him.

The beautiful and romantic heroine of Sir Egerton Brydges's novel has a library which contains works of the sentimental type as well as of a serious kind. 'There were all the best Poets, whose works are not mixed with impurity, on her shelves; and Mrs Smith's delightful History of *The Orphan of the Castle*, lay on her table, and seemed often to have been wet with her tears.' The indiscriminate mixing of the scholarly and sentimental seems to reflect the taste of Brydges himself:

She understands French, and Italian thoroughly, and takes particular delight in Petrarch. She does not much enjoy the French

---

[1] *Pride and Prejudice*, chapter 8.   [2] *Mary de Clifford*, p. 198.

9-2

poetry. Among the English, after her favourites Spenser, Milton and Cowley, Thomson seems altogether to please her most, and of the elegant love-writers of the last century, she possesses fairly written out in MS many little delicate poems of Lovelace, (who I believe was related to the family,) some of them such as I do not recollect seeing in print. . .of Novels and Romances, she thinks the inimitable *Castle of Otranto* and the plaintive novels of *Mrs Smith* in which the truest pathos, and most exquisite description are united, so much superior to any others, that she will not bear to hear any thing else named with them. But she is indeed a Poetess herself.[1]

This illustrates the manner in which the sentimentality of *Mary de Clifford* mingles with the pedantry and pretentiousness of its author. Sir Egerton Brydges is constantly obtruding, inserting his own interests into the story, and finding in fiction a compensation for his own failure as a poet and for his general disappointment at the lack of success of his intellectual ambitions. He evidently felt that he could impress the ordinary novel reader, whereas in more serious forms of art or intellectual attainment, he could not hope to succeed. Jane Austen, taking herself much less seriously, and making much less of a parade of her intellectual interests and reading, impresses one in the end by the intelligence and tact of her delicate silences and nuances.

The hero of *Mary de Clifford* is shot through the heart in a duel with Sir Peter, who flees to the Continent. The heroine becomes insane and dies. The melodramatic end of the novel contrasts with the realism and sobriety of Jane Austen's climaxes, and is the final justification of fiction which is based upon incidents taken from ordinary everyday experience.

Brydges's novel *Fitz-Albini* gained notoriety and even caused scandal because it contained references to some of his neighbours. Jane Austen, in her letter about it to her sister Cassandra, says that this was the only work of which his family were ashamed, and continues:

these scruples, however, do not at all interfere with my reading it, you will easily believe. We have neither of us yet finished the first volume. My father is disappointed—I am not, for I expected

---

[1] *Mary de Clifford*, pp. 147–8.

nothing better. Never did any book carry more internal evidence of its author. Every sentiment is completely Egerton's. There is very little story, and what there is told in a strange, unconnected way. There are many characters introduced, apparently merely to be delineated. We have not been able to recognise any of them hitherto, except Dr and Mrs Hey and Mr Oxenden, who is not very tenderly treated.[1]

Such criticism tells one a good deal about Jane Austen's own intentions and methods. Her deliberate suppression of merely personal ideas resulted in impersonality, detachment, impartiality and an authentic portrayal of experience. She never allowed her interest in her characters to lead her to forget the all-importance of the story, and the necessity of planning its development with precision and care. Nothing is wasted in her fiction. The smallest incident and character count and there are no irrelevances. She, too, may have based some of her characters on people whom she had met. Some of the incidents in her novels may have been founded on experience. But once incorporated into the fiction, they were transformed. Jane Austen's novels, like the little villages with which she is often concerned, are self-contained units, related to the actual world, yet controlled and shaped by art. Her letter suggests that she knew Sir Samuel well in life and through his writings. He was, in fact, a potential character for one of her own novels.

There is a further reference to *Fitz-Albini* in her letters. She writes from Bath to Cassandra at Steventon on 11 June 1799,

I would not let Martha read 'First Impressions' again upon any account, and am very glad that I did not leave it in your power. She is very cunning, but I saw through her design; she means to publish it from memory, and one more perusal must enable her to do it. As for 'Fitzalbini', when I get home she shall have it, as soon as ever she will own that Mr Elliot is handsomer than Mr Lance, that fair men are preferable to black; for I mean to take every opportunity of rooting out her prejudices.[2]

In November 1797 *First Impressions*, the early version of *Pride and Prejudice*, had been offered to the publisher Cadell, but was

---

[1] *Jane Austen's Letters*, ed. R. W. Chapman, p. 32.   [2] *Ibid.* p. 67.

not accepted. Jane Austen would therefore have particular reason to be interested in the novel by the brother of her beloved friend, Mrs Lefroy. *Arthur Fitz-Albini* appeared in 1798 'and bears even in greater degree the autobiographical characteristic of *Mary de Clifford*'.[1] The estates of the hero are burdened by debts, as were those of Woodvile in the earlier novel. He and the heroine, Jane St Leger, are delicate and sentimental, and surrounded by 'heartless fox-hunting squires'.[2] Jane has a spiteful guardian, Mrs Bracey, who gives her such a shock on the eve of her wedding that she dies. The death of the hero inevitably follows. Generally speaking, characters and incidents in this novel are extremely melodramatic, and there does not appear to have been even sufficiently interesting material for satire for it to be of use to Jane Austen. No doubt, she disapproved of it too strongly even to consider the possibility of ridiculing it. Certainly, however, the heroine of Jane Austen's *Pride and Prejudice* reacts in a very different manner from that of the hyper-sensitive and easily frightened Jane St Leger. There is a general resemblance between Mrs Bracey and Lady Catherine de Bourgh, but they belong to a conventional type of character in fiction that goes back to Lady Davers in *Pamela*, and there is no reason to believe that there is a case of specific relationship.

On the other hand, it is possible that the name and character of Mr Collins in *Pride and Prejudice* were inspired by Sir Samuel himself, who 'began in 1806 a new and augmented edition of Collins's "Peerage of England", a work which was eventually published in 1812'.[3] Boswell quotes Collins's *Peerage*[4] in his *Life of Johnson*, which Jane Austen had read, and she refers to Collins's predecessor, Dugdale's *Baronetage*, in the opening of *Persuasion*. It is likely that she knew that Sir Samuel was working on the revision, even though it was only published the year

---

[1] Mary Katherine Woodworth, *The Literary Career of Sir Samuel Egerton Brydges*, p. 42.
[2] *Ibid.* p. 43.
[3] Warwick Wroth, 'Sir Samuel Egerton Brydges', *Dictionary of National Biography*.
[4] Boswell, *Life of Johnson*, The Globe Edition, p. 31.

before *Pride and Prejudice* appeared. He had clerical connections, and his pompous, self-important manner resembles that of Mr Collins. He was a snob, too, who had put forward a claim to the barony of Chandos.

It would be an ironical fate for the self-styled genius to be brought into a novel for a satirical purpose as he himself had done with others in *Fitz-Albini*. The style of his writing reminds one of Mr Collins's 'mixture of servility and self-importance'[1] in his letter which Mary Bennet (perhaps another significantly named character, meant to indicate a reference to the heroine of Brydges's first novel) thinks well expressed. Mr Collins showed 'the self-conceit of a weak head living in retirement':[2] in the same way, Brydges had retired to Denton Court in Kent. Mr Collins, like him, had gone to one of the universities, though 'he had merely kept the necessary terms, without forming at it any useful acquaintance'.[3] On the other hand, Mr Collins had been partly influenced by an illiterate and miserly father. There is, no doubt, no exact parallel intended. On the contrary, Jane Austen created a general and universal type, avoiding anything in the nature of a merely personal lampoon, which would cause offence as the characters in *Fitz-Albini* had done.

It is ironical, however, that Mary, alone of the Bennet family, should appreciate Mr Collins. She bears no relation to the beautiful and romantic heroine of Brydges's novel, but perhaps she is meant to indicate the type of young woman who could be expected to be interested in the pretentious, pompous author. 'Mary rated his abilities much higher than any of the others; there was a solidity in his reflections which often struck her, and though by no means so clever as herself, she thought that if encouraged to read and improve himself by such an example as hers, he might become a very agreeable character.'[4]

The person whom Mr Collins does marry is Elizabeth's intimate friend, Charlotte Lucas. If Mr Collins is a satire on Brydges, it is appropriate that his wife should have the Christian

---

[1] *Pride and Prejudice*, chapter 13.
[2] *Ibid.* chapter 15.
[3] *Ibid.*
[4] *Ibid.* chapter 22.

name of his favourite novelist, Charlotte Smith. Their marriage, however, as depicted in Jane Austen's novel, is far from a romantic one. It may be said to represent prudence and realism in personal relationships, as opposed to the false romanticism depicted in the novels of Charlotte Smith and Brydges himself. Charlotte Lucas is a sensible, intelligent young woman, not a personification of sensibility. She is a 'prudent, steady character',[1] 'one of the very few sensible women who would have accepted Mr Collins, or have made him happy if they had'.[2] Elizabeth considered that her friend had an excellent understanding—though she was not certain that she thought her marrying Mr Collins the wisest thing she ever did. There is a further satirical piquancy in that Sir Samuel did marry an Elizabeth Byrche, the niece of Thomas Barret of Lee Priory.

There does not appear to be any indication that Jane Austen read or satirized Sir Egerton Brydges's *The Ruminator*, which contained a series of moral, critical and sentimental essays, and appeared in 1813. She was in Kent, however, that year from 17 September to 13 November. Perhaps *Emma* should be viewed partly as self-mockery, an exercise in humility and modesty after the deflation of the pretentious Sir Samuel, while Sir Walter Elliot in *Persuasion* represents a return to the theme of snobbery treated in the character of Mr Collins, with a similar interest in ridiculing an over-concern with social precedence. Sir Edward Denham, in Jane Austen's unfinished novel, *Sanditon*, is an enthusiastic admirer of Richardson and had read more sentimental novels than agreed with him. His incoherent and passionately romantic utterances may be a last satirical glance at the absurdities of a novelist whose works embodied so many examples of the false taste which Jane Austen wished to avoid, and who rebuked readers that 'commend and peruse with avidity tales descriptive of mere ordinary and daily life, which they call natural, as if nothing was natural that was not vulgar, or at least familiar'.[3]

---

[1] *Pride and Prejudice*, chapter 24.   [2] *Ibid.* chapter 32.
[3] *Mary de Clifford*, 'The Preface'.

CONCLUSION

The study of Jane Austen's relationship to her predecessors enables one to see how she gathered together all that was best in the literature of the past that she knew. What she wrote was, in its turn, assimilated and transformed by her successors. She occupied a crucial point in the history of the novel, foreshadowing, in certain ways, the more direct concern with moral issues that was to be characteristic of the Victorian age, yet retaining an essentially eighteenth-century impartiality, detachment and scepticism. Though she was limited in the range of social reference in her fiction, her intellectual interests were sufficient for her needs, and there is a sense in which she knew more and accepted life more fully than some of her more experienced and learned successors. Edith Wharton noted that 'Jane Austen's delicate genius flourished on the very edge of a tidal wave of prudery. Already Scott was averting his eyes from facts on which the maiden novelist in her rectory parlour had looked unperturbed.'[1]

It is the rectory parlour which should, perhaps, receive the final stress, for it is there that Jane Austen received much of her education. It is this background which distinguishes the earlier novelist from Edith Wharton herself, who mentioned three important aspects of her own education, knowledge of modern languages, the stress on the importance of good manners, and 'a reverence for the English language as spoken according to the best usage'.[2] On the other hand, Henry James's sophisticated friend quotes an article on Conrad in which the critic writes that he 'had worshipped the English language all his life like a lover, but had never romped with her in the nursery'.[3] Both she and Jane Austen had been able to romp with language

---

[1] Edith Wharton, *The Writing of Fiction* (London, 1925), pp. 62–3.
[2] Edith Wharton, *A Backward Glance* (New York, 1934), p. 48.
[3] *Ibid.* p. 53.

in this sense, without being merely frivolous or childish. Each of them was, at the same time, what Henry James described himself as being, 'a critical, a non-naïf, a questioning, worrying reader',[1] while retaining all the vitality and spontaneity of the colloquial tongue. They treated their own work and that of others with the same paradoxical combination of enthusiasm and dispassionate, ironic detachment.

It is the strength of the woman novelist generally, perhaps, that she is less inclined to lose touch with life and ordinary human experience than her male counterpart. Jane Austen's novels certainly constitute a 'criticism of life'. In her works, as in her own life, personal relationships came first. Books and reading were of supreme importance, but they were a means to an end, the civilized life. They were never allowed to become a substitute for life itself.

Yet the reader of Jane Austen's novels is constantly reminded of the world of books, especially in the early burlesques and in *Northanger Abbey*, which are directly concerned with extravagant behaviour resulting from a false taste in reading. Characters are revealed in their reactions to the world of fiction as much as in their conduct and manners. For Jane Austen believed that mistaken behaviour, immorality, and lack of intelligence, as exemplified in reading, are connected with each other. In *Pride and Prejudice*, Mr Hurst is surprised at Elizabeth preferring reading to cards, while Mr Darcy cannot comprehend the neglect of a family library. On the other hand, Miss Bingley's declaration that 'there is no enjoyment like reading' is shown to be hypocritical when she chooses a book merely because it is the second volume of Mr Darcy's.

There are even more references to reading in *Mansfield Park*, which is almost too bookish in its atmosphere. Edmund Bertram educates the heroine as Jane Austen's eldest brother is said to have educated Jane herself.[2] In *Emma*, the reflections of Mr Knightley on the heroine's reading lists represent, perhaps,

---

[1] Percy Lubbock, *The Letters of Henry James* (London, 1920), vol. II, p. 346.
[2] J. E. Austen-Leigh, *Memoir of Jane Austen*, ed. R. W. Chapman, p. 12.

an astringent and self-critical reminiscence by the novelist. In *Persuasion*, Anne Elliot, who resembles Fanny Price in this respect as in others, is a great reader, and when feeling depressed recalls 'some tender sonnet, fraught with the apt analogy of the declining year, with declining happiness, and the images of youth and hope, and spring, all gone together'.[1] This 'poetical despondence' is soon counteracted, however, by the description of the ploughs at work and the farmer meaning to have spring again. Neither Captain Harville nor Captain Wentworth appears to be fond of books, though Captain Harville had fashioned very pretty shelves, filled with the books of the sentimental, melancholy and weak-willed Captain Benwick. In Jane Austen's last, unfinished novel, *Sanditon*, books and opinions about various writers, ranging from Richardson to Burns, are as important as ever in determining the reader's estimate of the intelligence of the different characters.

Though the exact extent of Jane Austen's reading can never be known—it is only recently that it has been suggested that the title of *Pride and Prejudice* may have been taken from Gibbon or Jeremy Taylor[2]—it is probably more comprehensive than has been suspected. Yet it had its limitations, and it would be a mistake to imply that Jane Austen was an intellectual of George Eliot's calibre. *Adam Bede* contains a reference to Taylor's *Holy Living and Dying*,[3] the hero himself having read it, but one could hardly imagine Jane Austen introducing it directly into her fiction. On the other hand, George Eliot is inclined to make her learning obtrusive in an unartistic manner that Jane Austen avoided. Apart from these differences, they shared a common literary tradition. George Eliot describes *Adam Bede* as 'my simple story',[4] implying a comparison with Mrs Inchbald's novel, which also influenced Jane Austen.

The first book of *Middlemarch*, with its contrast between the

[1] *Persuasion*, chapter 10.
[2] See letters in *The Times Literary Supplement*, 29 December 1961 and 26 January 1962.
[3] *Adam Bede*, book II, chapter 19. [4] *Ibid.* chapter 17.

two sisters, derives from Jane Austen, the symbol of the jewellery being related to Jane Austen's use of it in *Mansfield Park*. Casaubon is a character that Jane Austen never attempted, but Fanny Burney did, in Dr Orkborne.[1] Gwendolen Harleth is a spoilt child like Emma, and she also recalls Mary Crawford, who shared her delight in horse-riding, and Jane Fairfax who was musical. George Eliot defended herself against the charge of triviality in making such a fuss about her heroines, particularly when they were partly trivial, as Gwendolen Harleth was, with the words, 'in these delicate vessels is borne onward through the ages the treasure of human affection'.[2] Her words were repeated by Henry James in his preface to *The Portrait of a Lady*. Jane Austen, George Eliot and Henry James shared this interest in what is described in *Daniel Deronda* as the slender, insignificant thread in human history, 'this consciousness of a girl, busy with her small inferences of the way in which she could make her life pleasant'.[3] For them, it was a thing of supreme importance, and in the relationship between Jane Austen and her successors one sees reflected the significance that her fiction had for those writers who were sensitive, intelligent and delicate enough to adapt, transform and modify, as she had done with the writings of her predecessors.

[1] *Camilla*, book I, chapter 6.
[2] *Daniel Deronda*, book II, chapter 11.   [3] *Ibid.*

Books for Young Ladies

(i) Leonora's library, *The Spectator*, Thursday, 12 April 1711

Ogleby's *Virgil*. *Dryden*'s *Juvenal*. *Cassandra*. *Cleopatra*. *Astraea*. Sir *Isaac Newton*'s Works. The *Grand Cyrus*: with a Pin stuck in one of the middle Leaves. *Pembroke*'s *Arcadia*. *Lock* of Human Understanding: with a Paper of Patches in it. A Spelling Book. A Dictionary for the Explanation of hard Words. *Sherlock* upon Death. The fifteen Comforts of Matrimony. Sir *William Temple*'s Essays. Father *Malbranche*'s Search after Truth, translated into *English*. A Book of Novels. The Academy of Compliments. *Culpepper*'s Midwifery. The Ladies' Calling. Tales in Verse by Mr *Durfey*: Bound in Red Leather, gilt on the Back, and doubled down in several Places. All the Classick Authors in Wood. A Set of *Elzivers* by the same Hand. *Clelia*: Which opened of it self in the Place that describes two Lovers in a Bower. *Baker*'s Chronicle. Advice to a Daughter. The New *Atalantis*, with a Key to it. Mr *Steele*'s Christian Heroe. A Prayer Book: With a Bottle of *Hungary* Water by the side of it. Dr *Sacheverell*'s Speech. *Fielding*'s Tryal. *Seneca*'s Morals. *Taylor*'s Holy Living and Dying. *La Ferte*'s Instructions for Country Dances.

(ii) From Lady Sarah Pennington's *An Unfortunate Mother's Advice to Her Absent Daughters* (1761, rev. ed. 1825.)[1]

Mason on Self Knowledge. Economy of Human Life. Seneca's Morals. Epictetus. Cicero's Offices. Collier's Antonius. The Female Spectator. The Rambler. The Adventurer. The World. Cicero's Familiar Letters. Pliny's Letters. Hoadley's Sermons. Seed's Sermons. Sherlock's Sermons. Sterne's Sermons. Fordyce's Sermons. Rollin's Belles Lettres. Nature Displayed. The Spectator. The Guardian. Rollin's Ancient History. Kennet's Antiquities of Rome. Hooke's Roman History. Hume's History of England. Robertson's History of Scotland. Milton's Poetical Works. Pope's Ethic Epistles. Fitzosborne's Letters. Epistles for the Ladies. Freeman's Letters. Vicar of Wakefield. Telemachus. Salmon's Geographical Grammar. Potter's Antiquities of Greece. Pope's Homer. Thompson's Works. Young's Works. Mrs Rowe's Works.

[1] See Appendix II, p. 143.

Langhorne's Works. Moore's Fables for the Female Sex. Tales of the Genii. Cotton's Visions. Dodsley's Collection of Poems.

(iii) From Clara Reeve's *The Progress of Romance* (1785)

A Father's Instructions, by Dr Percival. A Father's Legacy, by Dr Gregory. Mrs Talbot's Meditations for every Day in the Week. Mrs Rowe's Letters, Moral and Entertaining. Mrs Chapone's Works. Mrs[1] H. More's Sacred Dramas, and Search after Happiness. Moore's Fables for the Female Sex. Galateo, or the Art of Politeness. The Lady's Preceptor. The Geographical Grammar. Lowth's English Grammar. The Spectator. The Guardian. The Adventurer. Rambler. The Connoisseur. Nature Displayed. Fontenelle's Plurality of Worlds. Telemachus. Travels of Cyrus. Theatre of Education, by Madame Genlis. Tales of the Castle, by the same. Richardson's Works. Fordyce's Sermons to Young Women. Mason on Self Knowledge. The Speaker, by Dr Enfield.

[1] *Sic.*

APPENDIX II

Lady Sarah Pennington's *An Unfortunate Mother's Advice to Her Absent Daughters* (1761)

Printed with *Letters on the Improvement of the Mind* and *A Father's Legacy*, London, 1825.

[p. 175] *Introduction:*

> 'I labour to diffuse the important good,
> Till this great truth by all be understood:—
> That all the pious duties which we owe
> Our parents, friends, our country, and our God;
> The seeds of every virtue here below,
> From discipline alone, and early culture, grow.' West.
>
> (Gilbert West, *Education, a poem*, 1751.)

[p. 184] ...there are many excellent forms of prayer already composed: amongst these, none that I know of, are equal to Dr Hoadley's, the late Bishop of Winchester, which I recommend to your perusal and use. In the preface to them, you will find better instructions on this head than I am capable of giving, and to these I refer you.

[p. 186] The best books which I have ever met with on the subject, are Bishop Hoadley's *Plain Account of the Nature and End of the Sacrament of the Lord's Supper*, and Nelson's *Great Duty of frequenting the Christian Sacrifice*. To the former are annexed the prayers which I before mentioned—these are well worthy your attentive perusal;

[pp. 189–92] Study *your own language* thoroughly, that you may speak correctly, and write grammatically; do not content yourself with the common use of words, which custom has taught you from the cradle, but learn from whence they are derived, and what are there (*sic*) proper significations. *French* you ought to be as well acquainted with as with *English*: and *Italian* might, without much difficulty, be added. Acquire a good knowledge of *History*—that of your own country first, then of the other European nations—read them not with a/view to amuse but to improve your mind—and to that end make reflections on what you have read, which may be useful to yourself, and will render your conversation agreeable to others. Learn so much of *Geography*, as to form a just idea of the situation of places mentioned in any author, and this will make history more entertaining to you.

It is necessary for you to be perfect in the *four first rules of Arithmetic*; more you can never have occasion for, and the mind should not be burdened with needless application. *Music* and *Drawing* are accomplishments well worth the trouble of attaining, if your inclination and genius lead to either; if not, do not attempt them, for it will be only much time and great labour unprofitably thrown away, it being next to impossible to arrive at any degree of perfection in those arts, by the dint of perseverance only, if a good ear and a native genius be wanting. The study of *Natural Philosophy* you will find both pleasing and instructive—pleasing from the continual new discoveries to be made of the innumerably various beauties of nature—a most agreeable gratification of that desire of knowledge wisely implanted in the human mind—and highly instructive, as those discoveries lead to the contemplation of the great Author of nature, whose wisdom and goodness so conspicuously shine through all his works, that it is impossible to reflect seriously on them without admiration and gratitude.

These, my dear, are but a few of those mental improvements I would recommend to you; indeed there is no branch of knowledge that your capacity is equal to, and which you have an opportunity of acquiring, that, I think, ought to be neglected. It has been objected against all female learning, beyond that of household economy, that it tends only to fill the minds of the sex with a conceited vanity which sets them above their proper business—occasions an indifference to, if not a total neglect of, their family affairs—and serves only to render / them useless wives and impertinent companions. It must be confessed, that some leading ladies have given but too much cause for this objection; and, could it be proved to hold good throughout the sex, it would certainly be right to confine their improvements within the narrow limits of the nursery, of the kitchen and the confectionary; but, I believe it will, upon examination, be found, that such ill consequences proceed chiefly from too great an imbecility of mind to be capable of much enlargement, or from a mere affectation of knowledge, void of all reality. Vanity is never the result of understanding; a sensible woman will soon be convinced, that all the learning her utmost application can make her mistress of, will be, from the difference of education, in many points, inferior to that of a schoolboy: this reflection will keep her always humble, and will be an effectual check to that loquacity, which renders some women such insupportable companions.

The management of all domestic affairs is certainly the proper business of women; and, unfashionably rustic as such an assertion may be thought, it is not beneath the dignity of any lady, however high her rank, to know how to educate her children, to govern her servants—how to order an elegant table with economy, and to manage her whole family with prudence, regularity, and method: if in these she is defective, whatever may be her attainments in any other kinds of knowledge, she will act out of character; and, by not moving in her proper sphere, she will become rather the object of ridicule than of approbation. But, I believe, it may with truth be affirmed, that the neglect of these domestic concerns has much more frequently proceeded from an exorbitant love of diversions—from a ridiculous fondness for dress and gallantry—or, from a mistaken pride that has placed such duties in a servile light, from whence they have been considered as fit only for the employment of dependents, and below the attention / of a fine lady, than from too great an attachment to mental improvements; yet, from whatsoever cause such a neglect proceeds, it is equally unjustifiable.

[pp. 197–210] The morning being always thus advantageously engaged, the latter part of the day, as I before said, may be given to relaxation and amusement; some of these hours may very agreeably and usefully be employed by entertaining books, a few of which, in the English language, I will mention to you as a specimen of the kind I would recommend to your perusal; and I will include some others, religious and instructive. . . .

[Now follows the list of books given in appendix 1.]

From these you may form a judgment of that sort of reading, which will be both useful and entertaining to you. I have named only those *Practical Sermons*, which, I thought, would more directly influence your conduct in life;—*our rule of faith* should be taken from the Scripture alone, which we must understand for ourselves;—the controverted opinions of others serve in general rather to puzzle than to improve the mind.

Novels and *Romances*, very few of them, are worth the trouble of reading; some of them perhaps do contain a few good morals, but they are not worth the finding where so much rubbish is intermixed. Their moral parts indeed are like small diamonds amongst mountains of dirt and trash, which, after you have found them, are too inconsiderable to answer the pains of coming at; yet, ridiculous as these fictitious tales generally are, they are so artfully managed as to excite an idle curiosity to see the conclusion, by which means the reader is drawn on, through a tiresome length of / foolish adventures, from which neither knowledge, pleasure, or profit, seldom can accrue, to the common catastrophe of a wedding. The most I have met with of these writings, to say no worse, it is little better than the loss of time to peruse—but some of them have more pernicious consequences; by drawing characters that never exist in life, by representing persons and things in a false and extravagant light, and by a series of improbable causes, bringing on impossible events, they are apt to give a romantic turn to the mind, which is often productive of great errors in judgment, and of fatal mistakes in conduct—of this I have seen frequent instances, and therefore advise you scarce ever to meddle with any of them.

In justice however to a late ingenious author, this letter must not be reprinted, without my acknowledging that, since the last edition was published, I have accidentally met with one exception to my general rule, namely, The Vicar of Wakefield; that novel is equally entertaining and instructive, without being liable to any of the objections that occasioned the above restriction. This possibly may not be the only unexceptionable piece of the kind, but, as I have not met with any other, amongst a number I have perused, a single instance does not alter my opinion of the sort of writing; and, I still think, the chance is perhaps a thousand to one against the probability of obtaining the smallest degree of advantage from the reading any of them, as well as that very few are to be found, from which much injury may not be received.

Works of the Needle, that employ the fancy, may, if they suit your inclination, be sometimes a pretty amusement....

The Theatre, which by the indefatigable labour of the inimitable Mr Garrick, has been brought to very great perfection, will afford you an equally rational and improving entertainment:—your judgment will not now be called in question, your un/derstanding affronted, nor will your modesty be offended by the indecent ribaldry of those authors, who, to their defect in wit, have added the want of good sense and of good manners. Faults of this kind, that, from a blamable compliance with a corrupted taste, have sometimes crept into the works of good writers, are, by his prudent direction, generally rectified or omitted on the stage; you may now see many of the best plays performed in the best manner: do not, however, go to any that you have not before heard the character of; be present only at those which are approved by persons of understanding and virtue, as calculated to answer the proper ends of the theatre, namely, that of conveying instruction in the most pleasing method. Attend to the sentiment, apply the moral, and then you cannot, I think, pass an evening in a more useful, or in a more entertaining diversion.

Dancing may take its turn as a healthful exercise, and as it is generally suitable to the taste and gaiety of young minds.

Part of the hours appropriated to relaxation must, of necessity, be less agreeably taken up in the paying and receiving visits of mere ceremony and civility; a tribute, by custom authorized, by good manners enjoined: in these, when the conversation is only insignificant, join in it with an apparent satisfaction; talk of the elegance of a birthday suit, the pattern of a lace, the judicious assortment of jewels, the cut of a ruffle, or the set of a sleeve, with an unaffected ease; not according to the rank they hold in your estimation, but proportioned to the consequence they may be of in the opinion of those you are conversing with. The great art of pleasing is to appear pleased with others: suffer not then an ill-bred absence of thought, or a contemptuous sneer, ever to betray a conscious superiority of understanding, always productive of ill-nature and dislike;—suit yourself to the capacity and to the taste of your company, when that taste is confined to harmless trifles; but, where it is so far depraved as to delight in cruel sarcasms on the absent, to be pleased with discovering the blemishes in a good character, or in repeating the greater faults of a bad one, religion and humanity in that case forbid the least degree of assent;—if you have not any knowledge of the persons thus unhappily sacrificed to envy or to malice, and consequently are ignorant as to the truth or falsehood of such expressions, always suspect them to be ill-grounded or at least greatly exaggerated; show your disapprobation by a silent gravity, and by taking the first opportunity to change the subject: but, where any acquaintance with the character in question gives room for defending it, let not an ill-timed complaisance prevail over justice,—vindicate injured innocence with all the freedom and warmth of an unrestrained benevolence; and, where the faults of the guilty will admit of palliation, urge all that truth can allow in mitigation of error: from this method, besides the pleasure arising from the consciousness of a strict conformity to the great rule of *doing as you would be done by*, you will also reap to yourself the benefit of being less frequently pestered with themes ever painful to a humane disposition. If, unfortunately, you have some acquaintance whose malevolence of heart no sentiment of virtue, no check of good manners, can restrain from those malicious sallies of ill-nature, to them let your visits be made as seldom and as short as decency will admit,—there being neither benefit nor satisfaction to be found in such company, amongst whom only cards may be introduced with any advantage: on this account it will be proper for you to know how to play at the games most in use, because it is an argument of great folly to engage in anything without doing it well; but this is a diversion which I hope you will have no fondness for, as it is in itself, to say no worse, a very insignificant amusement. /

With persons for whom you can have no esteem, good-breeding may oblige you to keep up an intercourse of ceremonious visits, but politeness enjoins not the length or frequency of them; here inclination may be followed without a breach of civility:—there is no tax upon intimacy, but from choice—and that choice should ever be founded on merit, the certainty whereof you cannot be too careful in previously examining—great caution is necessary not to be deceived by specious appearances; a plausible behaviour, often, upon a superficial knowledge, creates a prepossession in favour of particulars, who, upon a nearer view, may be found to have no claim to esteem: the forming a precipitant judgment sometimes leads into an unwary intimacy, which it may prove absolutely necessary to break off, and yet that breach may be with more innumerable inconveniences; nay, perhaps with very material and lasting ill consequences: prudence, therefore, here enjoins the greatest circumspection. Few people are capable of friendship, and still fewer have all the qualifications one would choose in a friend; the fundamental point is a virtuous disposition—but, to that should be added, a good understanding, solid judgment, sweetness of temper, steadiness of mind, freedom of behaviour, and sincerity of heart;—seldom are these to be found united—never make a bosom friend of any one greatly deficient in any. Be slow in contracting friendship, and invariably constant in maintaining it;—expect not many friends, but think yourself happy if, through life, you meet with one or two who deserve that name, and have all the requisites for the valuable relation: this may justly be deemed the highest blessing of mortality; uninterrupted health has the general voice, but, in my opinion, such an intercourse of friendship as much deserves the preference, as the mental pleasures, both in nature and degree, exceed the corporeal: the weakness, the pains of the body, may be inexpressibly alleviated by the conversation / of a person, by affection endeared, by reason approved—whose tender sympathy partakes your afflictions and shares your enjoyments—who is steady in the correction, but mild in the reproof of your faults—like a guardian angel, ever watchful to warn you of unforeseen danger, and, by timely admonition, to prevent the mistakes incident to human frailty and to self-partiality—this is the true office of friendship. With such a friend, no state of life can be absolutely unhappy; but, destitute of such connexion, Heaven has so formed our natures for this intimate society, that amidst the affluence of wealth, and in the flow of un-interrupted health, there will be an aching void in the solitary nest, which can never otherwise know a plenitude of happiness. Should the Supreme Disposer of all events bestow on you this superlative gift—to such a friend let your heart be ever unreservedly open; con-ceal no secret thought; disguise no latent weakness; but bare your bosom to the faithful probe of honest friendship, and shrink not if it smarts beneath the touch; nor with tenacious pride dislike the person that freely dares to condemn some favourite foible; but, ever open to conviction, hear with attention, and receive with gratitude, the kind reproof that flows from tenderness: when sensible of a fault, be ingenuous in the confession—be sincere and steady in the correc-tion of it.

Happy is her lot, who, in a husband, finds this invaluable friend! yet so great is the hazard, so disproportioned the chances, that I could almost wish the dangerous die was never to be thrown for any of you! but, as probably it may, let me conjure ye all, my dear girls, if any of you take this most important step in life, to proceed with the utmost care, and with deliberate circumspection. Fortune and family it is the sole province of your father to direct in; he certainly has always an undoubted right to a negative voice, though not to a compulsive one: as a child is very / justifiable in the refusal of her hand, even to the absolute command of a father, where her heart cannot go with it, so is she extremely culpable in giving it contrary to his approbation:—here I must take shame to myself! and, for this unpardonable fault, I do justly acknowledge, that the subsequent ill consequences of a most unhappy marriage were the proper punish-ment: this, and every other error in my own conduct, I do, and shall, with the utmost candour, lay open to you, sincerely praying that you may reap the benefit of my experience, and that you may avoid those rocks, which, either by carelessness, or sometimes, alas! by too much caution, I have split against!—but to return—the chief point to be regarded in the choice of a *companion for life*, is a really virtuous principle—an unaffected goodness of heart; without this, you will be continually shocked by indecency, and pained by im-piety. So numerous have been the unhappy victims to the ridiculous opinion, *A reformed libertine makes the best husband*, that, did not experience daily evince the contrary, one would believe it impossible for a girl, who has a tolerable degree of understanding, to be made the dupe of so erroneous a position, which has not the least shadow of reason for its foundation, and which a small share of observation will prove to be false in fact. A man who has been long conversant with the worst sort of women is very apt to contract a bad opinion of, and a contempt for, the sex in general; incapable of esteeming any, he is suspicious of all;—jealous without cause—angry without provocation, and his own disturbed imagination is a continual source of ill-humour: to this is frequently joined a bad habit of body, the natural consequence of an irregular life, which gives an additional sourness to the temper. What rational prospect of happiness can there be with such a companion?—and that this is the general character of those who are called reformed rakes, obser/vations will certify; but, admit there be some exceptions, it is a hazard upon which no considerate woman would venture the peace of her whole future life. The vanity of those girls, who believe themselves capable of working miracles of this kind, and who give up their persons to men of libertine principles, upon the wild expectation of reclaiming them, justly deserves the disappointment which it will generally meet with; for, believe me, a wife is, of all persons, the least likely to succeed in such an attempt. Be it your care to find that virtue in a lover which you must never hope to form in a husband. Good sense and good nature are almost equally requisite; if the former is wanting, it will be next impossible to esteem the person of whose behaviour you may have cause to be ashamed—and mutual esteem is as necessary to happiness in the married state, as mutual affection; without the latter, every day will bring with it some fresh cause of vexation, till repeated quarrels produce a coldness which will settle into an irreconcileable aversion; and you will become, not only each other's torment, but the object of contempt to your family and to your acquaintance.

This quality of good nature is, of all others, the most difficult to be ascertained, on account of the general mistake of blending it with good humour, as if they were of themselves the same; whereas, in fact, no two principles of action are more essentially different—and this may require some explanation. By good nature, I mean that true benevolence which partakes the felicity of mankind, which promotes the satisfaction of every individual within the reach of its ability, which relieves the distressed, comforts the afflicted, diffuses blessings, and communicates happiness, as far as its sphere of action can extend; and which, in the private scenes of life, will shine conspicuous in the dutiful son, in the affectionate husband, the indulgent father, the faithful friend, and in the compassionate master, both to man and beast: whilst good hu/mour is nothing more than a cheerful pleasing deportment, arising either from a natural gaiety of mind, or from an affectation of popularity, joined to an affability of behaviour—the result of good breeding, and a ready compliance with the taste of every company: this kind of mere good humour is, by far, the most striking quality; it is frequently mistaken for, and complimented with, the superior name of real good nature: a man, by this specious appearance, has often acquired that appellation, who, in all the actions of his private life, has been a morose, cruel, revengeful, sullen, haughty tyrant.—Let them put on the cap whose temples fit the galling wreath! On the contrary, a man of a truly benevolent disposition, and formed to promote the happiness of all around him, may sometimes, perhaps, from an ill habit of body, an accidental vexation, or from a commendable openness of heart, above the meanness of disguise, be guilty of little sallies of peevishness, or of ill humour, which carrying the appearance of ill nature, may be unjustly thought to proceed from it, by persons who are un-acquainted with his true character, and who take ill humour and ill nature to be synonymous terms: though in reality they have not the least analogy to each other. In order to the forming a right judgment, it is absolutely necessary to observe this distinction, which will effectually secure you from the dangerous error of taking the shadow for the substance—an irretrievable mistake, pregnant with innumerable consequent evils!

From what has been said, it plainly appears, that the criterion of this amiable virtue is not to be taken from the general opinion;—mere good humour being, to all intents and purposes, sufficient, in this particular, to establish the public voice in favour of a man utterly devoid of every humane and benevolent affection of heart. It is only from the less conspicuous scenes of life, the more retired sphere of action, from the artless tenor of domestic conduct, that the real character can, with any cer/tainty, be drawn—these, un-disguised, proclaim the man; but, as they shun the glare of light, nor court the noise of popular applause, they pass unnoted—and are seldom known till after an intimate acquaintance: the best method, therefore, to avoid the deception in this case is, to lay no stress on outward appearances, which are too often fallacious, but to take the rule of judging from the simple unpolished sentiments of those, whose dependent connexions give them an undeniable certainty—who not only see, but who hourly feel, the good or bad effects of that disposition, to which they are subjected. By this, I mean, that if a man is equally respected, esteemed, and beloved by his tenants, by his dependents and domestics—from the substantial farmer to the laborious peasant—from the proud steward to the submissive wretch, who, thankful for employment, humbly obeys the menial tribe; you may justly conclude, he has that true good nature, that real benevolence, which delights in communicating felicity, and enjoys the satisfaction it diffuses; but if, by these, he is despised and hated—served merely from a principle of fear, devoid of affection—which is very easily discoverable, whatever may be his public character, however favourable the general opinion, be assured, that his disposition is such as can never be productive of domestic happiness. I have been the more particular on this head, as it is one of the most essential qualifications to be regarded, and of all others the most liable to be mistaken.

Never be prevailed with, my dear, to give your hand to a person defective in these material points: secure of virtue, of good nature, and understanding, in a husband, you may be secure of happiness—without the two former it is unattainable—without the latter, in a tolerable degree, it must be very imperfect.

Remember, however, that infallibility is not the property of man, or you may entail disappointment on yourself, by expecting what is never to be found; / —the best men are sometimes inconsistent with themselves:—they are liable to be hurried, by sudden starts of passion, into expressions and actions which their cooler reason will condemn;—they may have some oddities of behaviour, some peculiarities of temper;—they may be subject to accidental ill humour, or to whimsical complaints: blemishes of this kind often shade the brightest character, but they are never destructive of mutual felicity, unless when they are made so by an improper resentment, or by an ill-judged opposition. Reason can never be heard by passion—the offer of it tends only to inflame the more; when cooled, and in his usual temper, the man of understanding, if he has been wrong, will suggest to himself all that could be urged against him; the man of good nature will, upbraided, own his error; —immediate contradiction is, therefore, wholly unserviceable and highly imprudent,—an after-repetition, equally unnecessary and injudicious. Any peculiarities in the temper or behaviour ought to be properly represented in the tenderest and in the most friendly manner; and, if the representation of them is made discreetly, it will generally be well taken: but, if they are so habitual as not easily to be altered, strike not too often upon the unharmonious string—rather let them pass as unobserved: such a cheerful compliance will better cement your union; and they may be made easy to yourself, by reflecting on the superior good qualities by which these trifling faults are so greatly over-balanced. You must remember, my dear, these rules are laid down, on the supposition of your being united to a person who possesses the three essential qualifications for happiness before mentioned; in this case, no farther direction is necessary but that you strictly perform the duty of a wife—namely to love, to honour, and obey;—the two first articles are a tribute so indispensably due to merit, that they must be paid by inclination, and they naturally lead to the performance of the last, which will not only be / an easy, but a pleasing task,—since nothing can ever be enjoined by such a person that is in itself improper; and few things will, that can, with any reason, be disagreeable to you. Here should this subject end, were it not more than possible for you, after all that has been urged, to be led, by some inferior motive, to the neglect of the primary caution; and that, either from an opinion too hastily entertained, from an unaccountable partiality, or from the powerful prevalence of persuasion, you may be unfortunately induced to give your hand to a man, whose bad heart and morose temper, concealed by a well-practised dissimulation, may render every flattering hope of happiness abortive.—May Heaven, in mercy, guard you from this fatal error!—Such a companion is the worst of all temporal ills; a deadly potion, that imbitters every social scene of life, damps every rising joy, and banishes that cheerful temper, which alone can give a true relish to the blessings of mortality:—most sincerely do I pray that this may never be your lot! and, I hope, your prudent circumspection will be sufficient to guard you from the danger: but the bare possibility of the event makes it not unnecessary to lay down a few rules for the maintaining some degree of ease, under such a deprivation of happiness. This is by far the most difficult part of my present undertaking; it is hard to advise here, and still harder to practise the advice; the subject also is too extensive to be minutely treated within the compass of *a letter*, which must confine me to the most material points only; in these, I shall give you the best directions in my power, very ardently wishing, that you may never have occasion to make use of them.

The being united to a man of irreligious principles makes it impossible to discharge a great part of the proper duty of a wife....

[pp. 225–6] ...To enumerate all the social duties would lead me too far; suffice it, therefore, my dear, in a few words to sum up what remains; let truth ever dwell upon your tongue; scorn to flatter any, and despise the person who would practise so base an art upon yourself. Be honestly open in every part of your behaviour and conversation. All, with whom you have any intercourse, even down to the / meanest station, have a right to civility and good humour from you: a superiority of rank or fortune is no license for a proud supercilious behaviour, the disadvantages of a dependent state are alone sufficient to labour under; it is both unjust and cruel to increase them, either by a haughty deportment, or by the unwarrantable exercise of a capricious temper.

Aim at perfection, or you will never reach to an attainable height of virtue. Be religious without hypocrisy, pious without enthusiasm. Endeavour to merit the favour of God, by a sincere and uniform obedience to whatever you know, or believe to be His Will. . . .

APPENDIX III

Mrs Jane West: *Letters to a Young Lady: in which the duties and character of women are considered chiefly with a reference to prevailing opinions.*

The Fourth Edition. In Three Volumes.
London, 1811.

VOL. III, LETTER XI. ON CONVERSATION, SOCIETY AND FRIENDSHIP

[pp. 37–46] Conversation resembles, in many particulars, a game of chance. The best players are those who, still keeping in view the established rules, adapt themselves to accidental variations with skill and adroitness. Whoever engages in it with a steadfast resolution of making particular strokes, or ties himself down by / a preconcerted manner, will be sure to lose; and he who resolves to keep the game in his own hands plays unfairly. 'A civil guest,' says the old poet, 'will neither talk all nor eat all the feast.' When we talk, let us consider rather what will be *requisite* for us to say, than what we shall be gratified in saying. After keeping the ball in our hand a due time, let us resign it to another player, and only occasionally catch it in its rebound. But let us, in that case, beware of arresting it by too hard a blow. Petty contradictions are not the spur, but the quietus, of agreeable conversation. They proceed from a habit formed in early life, to which parents in the middle ranks of society are never sufficiently attentive. If half the pains that are taken in teaching young women accomplishments were bestowed on the regulation of their tempers, and the improvement of their/manners, our social pleasures would receive most valuable improvements. It is to be lamented, that this most teasing habit often distinguishes very worthy people, who adopt it from a mistaken regard to truth and sincerity. As these are especially apt to suppose that a domestic party releases every body from all restraints, they frequently contrive to convert a family meeting into a battle royal; somewhat resembling the contest of a brood of turkey pouts in which everyone gets pecked, and none discover for what reason. The most miserable fate, however, awaits a stranger, who, supposing this engagement to proceed from secret enmity, unfortunately interferes to restore peace, and does not, till after he has received the rebuffs of *every* combatant, discover that they were all the while *cackling* in perfect friendship. This humour generally breaks out in / the midst of some narrative, in which the repeater is interrupted with something quite as unessential as Miss Carolina Wilhelmina Amelia Skegg's elucidations of Lady Blarney's crim. con. story, in the Vicar of Wakefield; and as both parties instantly quit the main point, to ascertain the verity of the appendage, all the spirit of the tale (if it ever had any) instantly evaporates, and leaves the combatants to fight over a dead body, like the heroic Greeks and magnanimous Trojans. A love of detailing wonders (another lamentable fault in conversation) is extremely apt to rouse this contradictious spirit, which really is a sort of wildfire very liable to agitation, irresistible in its progress, and incapable of extinction until it has consumed all the fuel within its reach. It is not always harmless, unless it is kindled among the weeds which / overrun a rich but neglected soil. We may deduce family dissensions, breach of friendship, nay irreconciliable enmity, from this source, much oftener than we can ascribe these lamentable consequences to any great violations of the principles of morality.

Whenever, therefore, we feel inclined to deny what has just been advanced, let us previously reflect whether our motive for interference be such as will justify that interruption of general harmony which contradiction always endangers. Is the misrepresentation gross, is the mistake at once palpable and important? If so, a duty paramount to the laws of good-breeding compels us actively to support the cause of truth; but (even then) we should still recollect, that no cause is *well supported* without moderation and urbanity. There is no occasion for the loud scream of / reprobation; a hint is more forcible, if not to the offender, at least to the bystander. If the culprit refuses to receive this admonition, and even maintains her own opinion or statement with pertinacity, it will be more advisable to decline the contest, than to enter on, what is quite inimical to the nature of social converse, a long angry argument. Discussions of important points may sometimes be pursued in company with improvement or pleasure; but then the weapons of controversy must be wielded by masters of the science, who possess real command of temper as well as information, who can *gracefully* submit to *defeat* and who scorn to *pursue* a *victory* after it has been *acknowledged*. Such talents are too seldom found in unison, to induce me to rescind my affirmation, that contradiction and argument are the pests of conversation; and unfor/tunately the more insignificant the occasion, the more irritating are the consequences.

Giving unpleasant answers has been already alluded to; bitter irony is another solecism of the rules of politeness. To say what you are certain will give unnecessary pain, is not only a breach in manners but in morals. If Wit be restrained by the fundamental laws of her own empire from lacerating by her keenness, shall the usurper Dulness be allowed to use her mallet, to do what the bright daughter of Fancy renounces her legitimacy by attempting! Rude sarcasms might always be corrected by the company before whom the offence is committed. If there were no *thoughtless* laughers, there would be no *offensive* jesters. The leaven of vanity operates in this instance, as it does in most of our petty faults. Solicitous of distinction, yet ignorant of worthy means to procure / it, the splenetic dullard resolves to be celebrated, though it be only as the *destroyer* of that comfort which he cannot *promote*. Banishment to Coventry would be a deserved and salutary punishment; nothing can sooner reclaim malignity than to show its own insignificance. But, to undertake the execution of this sentence, requires more hardihood than generally accords with the female character.

An adept in the practice of christian candour knows that we must invariably conform to the precept of 'thinking no evil'. Among the minute but highly important ramifications of this extensive duty, we may rank all unpleasant constructions of the words of our associates: and, when they really will bear no other interpretation, endeavouring to show the speaker that we are desirous of understanding them in a favourable light. A good-humoured answer to a splenetic remark constitutes those 'soft words' which Solomon commends; and there are few tempers so truly diabolical but will yield, if not to the suavity, at least to the address of gentle management; I except passionate people, who, if they are generous (the usual concomitant of warmth) are always soonest vanquished, by showing them that the darts they throw about at *random* make *painful* wounds.

The precept of 'in honour preferring one another', will teach us a habit extremely gratifying to all with whom we associate: I mean that of appearing interested in their affairs. This species of attention is especially due to those who are in affliction or perplexity. We cannot expect that people who are so circumstanced can enter into the ordinary style of conversation with ease and cheerfulness; and, it is probable, we have no other way of softening their calamities than by taking an interest / in their affairs.

William Gilpin: *An Essay upon Prints:* containing remarks upon the principles of picturesque beauty, the different kinds of prints, and the characters of the most noted masters; illustrated by criticisms upon particular pieces; to which are added, some cautions that may be useful in collecting prints. London, 1768.

[p. 1] *Explanation of Terms.*

Composition, in its *large* sense, means a picture in general: in its *limited* one, the art of grouping figures, and combining the parts of a picture. In this latter sense it is synonymous with *disposition.*

Design, in its strict sense, applyed chiefly to *drawing*: in its more enlarged one, defined page 3. In its most enlarged one, sometimes taken for a picture in general.

A whole: The idea of *one* object, which a picture should give in its comprehensive views.

[p. 2] *Expression*: its strict meaning defined page 24: but it often means the force, by which objects of *any* kind are represented.

Effect arises chiefly from the management of light; but the word is sometimes applied to the general view of a picture.

Spirit, in its strict sense, defined p. 34, but it is sometimes taken in a more inlarged one, and means the *general* effect of a masterly performance.

Manner, synonymous with *execution.*

Picturesque: a term expressive of that peculiar kind of beauty, which is agreeable in a picture.

[p. 3] *Picturesque grace*: an agreeable form given, in a picture, to a clownish figure.

Repose, or *quietness* applyed to a picture, when the whole is harmonious; when nothing glares either in the light, shade, or colouring.

To *keep down, take down,* or *bring down,* signify throwing a degree of shade upon a glaring light.

A middle tint, a medium between a strong light, and strong shade: the phrase is not at all expressive of colour.

Catching lights: strong lights, which strike upon some particular parts of an object, the rest of which is in shadow.

Studies, the scetched (*sic*) ideas of a painter, not wrought into a whole.

Freedom, the result of quick execution.

Extremities, hands and feet.

Air, expresses chiefly the graceful action of the head; but often means a graceful attitude.

Contrast, the opposition of one part to another.

I. CHAPTER I. THE PRINCIPLES OF PAINTING CONSIDERED, SO FAR AS THEY RELATE TO PRINTS

[pp. 2–3] ...we consider a print, as we do a picture, in a double light, with regard to a *whole*, and with regard to its parts.

To make a print agreeable as a *whole*, a just observance of those rules is necessary, which relate to *design, disposition, keeping*, and the *distribu/tion of light*: to make it agreeable in its *parts*, of those which relate to *drawing, expression, grace*, and *perspective*.

By *design* (a term which painters sometimes use in a more limited sense) I mean the general conduct of the piece as a representation of such a particular story. It answers, in an historical relation of a fact, to a judicious choice of circumstances, and includes a *proper time, proper characters, the most affecting manner of introducing those characters*, and *proper appendages*.

[pp. 3–4] With regard to a *proper time*, the painter is assisted by good old dra/matic rules; which inform him, that *one* point of time only should be taken—the most affecting in the action; and that no other part of the story should interfere with it. ...

With regard to *characters*, the painter must suit them to his *piece* by attending to historical truth, if his subject be history; or to heathen mythology, if it be fabulous.

[p. 5] He must farther *introduce them properly*. They should be ordered in such an advantageous manner, that the principal figures, those which are most concerned in the action, should catch the eye *first*, and engage it *most*. This is an essential ingredient in a well-told story. In the first place, they should be the least embarrassed of the group. This alone gives them distinction. But they may be farther distinguished, sometimes by a *broad light*; sometimes, tho' but rarely, and when the subject requires it, by a *strong shadow*, in the midst of the light; sometimes by a remarkable *action* or *expression*; and sometimes by a combination of two or three of these modes of distinction.

APPENDIX IV

[pp. 6–7] The last thing included in design is the use of *proper appendages*. By *appendages* are meant animals, landskip, buildings, and in general, what ever is introduced into the piece by way of ornament. Every thing of this kind should correspond with the subject, and rank in a proper subordination to it. BASSAN would sometimes paint a scripture-story; and his method was, to crowd his foreground with cattle, well painted indeed, but wholly foreign to his subject; while you seek for his principal figures, and at length perhaps with difficulty find them in some remote corner of his picture. We often see a landskip well adorned with a story in miniature. The *landskip* here is principal; but at the / same time the figures, which tell the story, tho' subordinate to the landskip, are the *principal figures*. BASSAN'S practice was different. In his pictures neither the *landskip*, nor the *story* is principal. His cattle are the ornament of his pieces. To introduce a story then is absurd.

When all these rules are observed, when a proper point of time is chosen; when characters corresponding with the subject are introduced, and these ordered so judiciously as to point out the story in the strongest manner; and lastly, when all the appendages, and under-parts of the piece are suitable, and subservient to the subject, then the story is well told, and of course the design is perfect.

[pp. 8–10] The second thing to be considered with regard to a *whole* is *disposition*. By this word is meant the art of grouping the figures, and of combining the several parts of a picture. *Design* considers how each part, *separately taken*, concurs in producing a *whole*—a *whole*, arising from the *unity of the subject*, not the *effect of the object*. For the figures in a piece may be so ordered, as to tell the story in an affecting manner, which is as far as *design* goes, and yet may want that agreeable *combination*, which is necessary to please the eye. To produce such a combination is the business of *disposition*. In the cartoon of St. Paul *preaching at Athens*, the *design* is perfect; and / the characters, in particular, are so ordered, as to tell the story in a very affecting manner; yet the several parts of the picture are far from being agreeably combined. If RUBENS had had the *disposition* of the materials of this picture, and the management of the lights, it's effect as a *whole* had been very different. Having thus distinguished between *design* and *disposition*, I shall explain the latter a little farther.

It is an obvious principle, that one object at a time is enough to engage either the senses or the intellect. Hence the necessity of *unity* or a *whole* in painting. The eye, upon a complex view, must be able to / comprehend the picture as *one object*, or it cannot be satisfyed. It may be pleased indeed by feeding on the parts separately; but a picture, which can please no otherwise; is as poor a production, as a machine, the springs and wheels of which are finished with nicety, but are unable to act in concert, and effect the intended movement.

[pp. 10–11] Now *disposition*, or the art of grouping and combining the figures, and several parts of a picture is an essential, which contributes greatly to produce a *whole* in painting. When the parts are scattered, they have no dependance on each other; they are still only parts: but by an agreeable / grouping, they are massed together, and become a *whole*.

In disposing figures great artifice is necessary to make each group open itself in such a manner, as to set off advantageously the several figures, of which it is composed. The *action* at least of each figure should appear.

No group can be agreeable without *contrast*. By *contrast* is meant the opposition of one part to another. A sameness in attitude, action or expression, among figures in the same group, will always disgust the eye. In the cartoon of ST PAUL *preaching at Athens*, the contrast among the figures is incomparably fine....

[pp. 12–13] Nor indeed is *contrast* required only among the *figures* of the *same* group, but also among the *groups themselves*, and among *all the parts*, of which the piece is composed. In the *beautiful gate of the temple*, the figures of the principal group are very well contrasted; but the adjoining group is disposed almost in the same manner; which, together with the formal pillars, introduce a disagreeable regularity into the picture.

The judicious painter, however, whether he group, combine, or con/trast ,will always avoid the *appearance of artifice*. The several parts of his picture will be so suited to each other, that his art will seem the result of chance. In the *sacrifice at Lystra*...altho' the figures are disposed with the utmost art, they appear with all the ease of nature. The remaining part of the group is an instance of the reverse, in which a number of heads appear manifestly stuck in to fill up vacuities.

[pp. 14–15] But farther, as a *whole*, or *unity*, is an essential of beauty, *that disposition* is certainly the most perfect which admits but *one* group. All subjects, however, will not allow this *close* observance of unity. When this is the case, the several groups must again be combined, chiefly by a proper distribution of light, so as [to] constitute a *whole*.

But as the *whole* will soon be lost, if the constituent *parts* become *numerous*, it follows, that *many* groups must not be admitted. Judicious painters have thought *three* the utmost number, that can be allowed. Some subjects indeed, as battles, and triumphs, necessarily require a great number of figures, and of course / various combinations of groups. In the management of *such* subjects, the greatest art is necessary to preserve a *whole*. Confusion in the figures must be expressed without confusion in the picture. A writer should treat his subject *clearly*, tho' he write upon obscurity.

With regards to *disposition*, I shall only add, that the *shape* or *form* of the group should also be considered. The *triangular* form MICHAEL ANGELO thought the most beautiful. And indeed there is a lightness in it, which no other form can receive.

[pp. 16–18] . . . The triangular form too is capable of the most variety: for the vertical angle of a group so disposed may either be acute, or obtuse, in any degree. . . . The cartoons afford few instances of beauty in the *forms of groups*. In the works of Salvator Rosa we frequently find them.

The painter, when he hath chosen his subject, should always scetch out some beautiful form of grouping, which may best suit it; within which bounds he should, as nearly as may / be, without affectation, confine his figures. What I mean is, that the *form* of the group should never be left at random.

A third thing to be considered in a picture, with regard to *a whole*, is *keeping*. This word implies the different degrees of strength and faintness, which objects receive from nearness and distance. A nice observance of the gradual fading of light and shade contributes greatly towards the production of *a whole*. Without it, the distant parts, instead of being connected with the objects at hand, appear like foreign objects, wildly introduced, and unconnected. Diminished in *size* only, they put you in / mind of Lilliput and Brobdingnag united in one scene. *Keeping* is generally found in great perfection in DELLA BELLA's prints; and the want of it as conspicuously in TEMPESTA's.

Nearly allied to *keeping* is the doctrine of *harmony*, which equally contributes towards the production of a *whole*. In *painting*, the practice of this doctrine has amazing force. A judicious arrangement of according tints will strike even the unpracticed eye. The *effect* of every picture, in a great measure, depends on one principal and master-tint, which prevails over the whole.

[p. 19] . . . Of this ruling tint, whatever it is, every object in the picture should in a degree participate. This theory is founded on principles of truth, and produces a fine effect from the *harmony*, in which it unites every object.—But altho' *harmony* shews its effect chiefly in *painting*, yet in some measure the effect of *prints* may be assisted by it. Unless they are harmonized by the same *tone of shadow*, if I may so express myself, there will always appear a great deficiency in them. By the same *tone of shadow*, I mean not only the *same manner* of execution, but an *uniform* degree of strength.

[p. 20] *Keeping* then proportions a proper degree of strength to the near and distant parts, in respect to *each other*. *Harmony* goes a step farther, and keeps each part quiet, with respect to itself, and the *whole*. I shall only add, that in scetches, and rough etchings, no *harmony* is expected: it is enough, if *keeping* be observed. Harmony is looked for only in finished compositions. If you would see the want of it in the strongest light, examine a worn-print, harshly retouched by some bungler.

The last thing, which contributes to produce a *whole*, is a proper *distribution of light*.

[p. 23] Having thus considered those essentials of a print, which produce a *whole*, it remains to consider those, which relate to the *parts—drawing, expression, grace,* and *perspective*. With regard to these, let it be first observed, that, in order, they are inferior to the other. The production of a *whole* is the great effect, that should be aimed at in a picture: a picture without a *whole* is properly only a study: and those things, which produce a *whole* are of course the *principal* foundation of beauty.

[p. 28] I say the less on this subject, as it hath been so well explained by the ingenious author of the *Analysis of Beauty*.

Thus *contrast* is the foundation of *grace*; but it must ever be remembered, that contrast should be accompanied with *ease*. The body should be *turned*, not *twisted*; every *constrained* posture avoided; and every motion such, as nature, which loves ease, would dictate.

[p. 29] I shall only observe farther, that when the piece consists of many figures, the contrast of *each single* figure should be subordinate to the contrast of the *whole*.

[p. 30] *Perspective* is that proportion, with regard to *size*, which near and distant objects, with their parts, bear to each other. It answers to *keeping*: one gives the outline; and the other fills it up. Without a competent knowledge of *perspective* very absurd things would be introduced: and yet to make a vain shew of it is pedantic. —Under this head may be reduced fore-shortning.

[p. 31] By *execution* is meant that manner of working, by which each artist produces his effect. Artists may differ in their *execution* or *manner*, and yet all excel.

CHAPTER II: OBSERVATIONS ON THE DIFFERENT
KINDS OF PRINTS

[p. 49] There are three kinds of prints, *engravings*, *etchings*, and metzotintos. The characteristic of the first is *strength*; of the second *freedom*; and of the third, *softness*.

[p. 54] *Mere engravers*, in general, are little better than *mere mechanics*.

[p. 55] *Etching*, on the other hand, is more particularly adapted to scetches, and slight designs; which, if executed by an engraver, would entirely lose their freedom; and with it their beauty. Landskip too, in general, is the object of *etching*. The foliage of trees, ruins, sky, and indeed every part of landskip requires the utmost freedom. In finishing an etched landskip with the *tool* (as it is called) too much care cannot be taken to prevent heaviness.

[p. 56] ...in landskip the business is peculiarly delicate.

An *engraved* plate, unless it be cut very slightly, will cast off five hundred good impressions. An *etched* one will not give above two hundred; unless it be eaten very deep, and then it may perhaps give three hundred.

CHAPTER III: CHARACTERS OF THE MOST NOTED MASTERS.
MASTERS IN HISTORY. MASTERS IN LANDSKIP

[pp. 168–9] Our celebrated countryman Hogarth cannot properly be omitted in a catalogue of engravers; and yet he ranks in none of the foregoing classes. With this apology I shall introduce him here.

The works of this master abound in the true humour; and satyr, which is generally well-directed: they are admirable moral lessons, and a fund of entertainment suited to every taste; a circumstance, which shews them to be just copies of nature. We may consider them too as valuable repositories of the manners, customs, and dresses of the present age. What a fund of entertainment would a col/lection of this kind afford, drawn from every period of Britain?— How far the works of HOGARTH will bear a *critical examination*, may be the subject of a little more enquiry.

In *design* HOGARTH was seldom at a loss. His invention was fertile; and his judgment accurate. An improper incident is rarely introduced; a proper one rarely omitted. No one could tell a story better; or make it, in all its circumstances, more intelligible. His genius, however, it must be owned, was suited only to *low*, or *familiar* subjects. It never soared above *common* life: to subjects naturally sublime: or which from antiquity, or other incidents borrowed dignity, he could not rise.

[p. 170] In *composition* we see little in him to admire.

[p. 171] ...of the *distribution of light* HOGARTH had as little knowledge as of *composition*....Neither was HOGARTH a master in *drawing*.

[p. 172] The author of the *Analysis of beauty*, it might be supposed, would have given us more instances of *grace*, than we find in the works of HOGARTH; which shews strongly that theory and practice are not always united.

[p. 173] With instances of picturesque grace his works abound.

But of his *expression*, in which the force of his genius lay, we cannot speak in terms too high.

CHAPTER IV: REMARKS ON PARTICULAR PRINTS

CHAPTER V: CAUTIONS IN COLLECTING PRINTS

BIBLIOGRAPHY

GENERAL

F. W. Bateson (ed.), *The Cambridge Bibliography of English Literature*, in 4 vols. (Cambridge, 1940), vol. v, *Supplement*, ed. George Watson (Cambridge, 1957).

Frank Gees Black, *The Epistolary Novel in the Late Eighteenth Century* (University of Oregon, 1940).

A. S. Collins, *Authorship in the Days of Johnson* (London, 1927).

—— *The Profession of Letters* (London, 1928).

Allene Gregory, *The French Revolution and the English Novel* (New York and London, 1915).

A. C. Kettle, *An Introduction to the English Novel*, vol. i (London, 1951).

F. R. Leavis, *The Great Tradition* (London, 1948).

Q. D. Leavis, *Fiction and the Reading Public* (London, 1932).

J. M. S. Tompkins, *The Popular Novel in England, 1770–1800* (London, 1932).

Annals of English Literature 1475–1950, ed. R. W. Chapman and others (Oxford, 1961).

J. E. Austen-Leigh, *Memoir of Jane Austen*, ed. R. W. Chapman (Oxford, 1951).

Mary Augusta Austen-Leigh, *Personal Aspects of Jane Austen* (London, 1920).

W. and R. A. Austen-Leigh, *Jane Austen, Her Life and Letters* (London, 1913).

Willi Bühler, *Die 'Erlebte Rede' im englischen Roman* (Zürich and Leipzig, n.d.).

R. W. Chapman, *Jane Austen, Facts and Problems* (Oxford, 1948).

Elizabeth Jenkins, *Jane Austen, a Biography* (London, 1949).

Mary Lascelles, *Jane Austen and Her Art* (Oxford, 1939).

Q. D. Leavis, 'A Critical Theory of Jane Austen's Writings', *Scrutiny*, vol. x (June and October 1941, and January 1942).

—— Introductions to *Mansfield Park* and *Sense and Sensibility* (with *Lady Susan* and *The Watsons*) (London, 1957, 1958).

C. S. Lewis, 'A Note on Jane Austen', *Essays in Criticism*, vol. iv, no. 4 (October 1954).

Robert Liddell, *The Novels of Jane Austen* (London, 1963).

G. E. Mitton, *Jane Austen and Her Times* (London, 1905).

Marvin Mudrick, *Jane Austen, Irony as Defense and Discovery* (Princeton, 1952).

C. L. Thomson, *Jane Austen, a Survey* (London, 1929).

J. M. S. Tompkins, 'Elinor and Marianne: A Note on Jane Austen', *The Review of English Studies*, vol. XVI (1940).

Léonie Villard, *Jane Austen, a French Appreciation*, and R. Brimley Johnson, *A New Study of Jane Austen* (London, 1924).

Andrew Wright, *Jane Austen's Novels*, revised edition (London, 1961).

PART I: THE GENERAL LITERARY TRADITION

Primary sources   Chapter 1: *Periodicals*

Addison and Steele, *The Tatler* (1709–11) and *The Spectator* (1711–14).

Dr Samuel Johnson, *The Rambler* (1750–2) and *The Idler* (1758–60). Contributions to *The Adventurer* (1753–4).

Secondary sources

John Bailey and L. F. Powell, *Dr Johnson and His Circle* (Oxford, 1947).

A. Beljame, *Men of Letters and the English Public 1660–1744* (1881), trans. E. O. Lorimer, ed. Bonamy Dobrée (London, 1948).

Dr Johnson, *Lives of the English Poets*, 'Joseph Addison'.

J. W. Krutch, *Samuel Johnson* (London, 1948).

Leslie Stephen, *English Literature and Society in the Eighteenth Century* (London, 1904).

W. K. Wimsatt, Jr., *The Prose Style of Samuel Johnson* (Oxford, 1941).

Primary sources   Chapter 2: *Moralists in prose*

Baldassare Castiglione, *The Book of the Courtier* (1528, trans. 1561).

Giovanni Della Casa, *Il Galateo* (1558, trans. 1576, 1701 and 1774).

La Bruyère, *Les Caractères de Théophraste avec Les Caractères ou Les Mœurs de ce Siècle* (1688).

George Savile, First Marquess of Halifax, *Advice to a Daughter* (1688).

Joseph Butler, *Fifteen Sermons* (1726).

William Law, *A Serious Call to a Devout and Holy Life* (1728).

Lady Sarah Pennington, *An Unfortunate Mother's Advice to her Absent Daughters* (1761).

James Fordyce, *Sermons to Young Women* (1766).

Mrs Chapone, *Letters on the Improvement of the Mind* (1773).

Dr Gregory, *A Father's Legacy to his Daughters* (1774).

Lord Chesterfield, *Letters to his Son* (1774).

Thomas Sherlock, *Several Discourses preached at the Temple Church* (1754–8 and 1797).

Hugh Blair, *Sermons* (1777–1801).

167

Dr Samuel Johnson, *Lives of the English Poets* (1783).

Thomas Gisborne, *An Enquiry into the Duties of Men in the higher and middle classes of Society in Great Britain, resulting from their respective Stations, Professions, and Employments* (1794).

——*An Enquiry into the Duties of the Female Sex* (1797).

Hannah More, *Strictures on the Modern System of Female Education* (1799).

Jane West, *Letters addressed to a Young Man* (1801).

—— *Letters to a Young Lady* (1806).

Hannah More, *Practical Piety* (1811), and *Christian Morals* (1813).

Secondary sources

Joyce Hemlow, 'Fanny Burney and the Courtesy Books', *P.M.L.A.* vol. LXV, no. 5 (September 1950).

M. G. Jones, *Hannah More* (Cambridge, 1952).

R. A. Knox, *Enthusiasm*, Oxford, 1950.

John E. Mason, *Gentlefolk in the Making* (Oxford, 1935).

David Spring, 'The Clapham Sect: Some Social and Political Aspects', *Victorian Studies*, vol. V, no. 1 (September 1961).

Primary sources   Chapter 3: The Picturesque

William Gilpin, *An Essay upon Prints* (1768).

—— *Observations on the River Wye, and several parts of South Wales, etc., relative chiefly to Picturesque Beauty: made in the summer of the year 1770* (1782).

—— *Observations, relative chiefly to Picturesque Beauty, made in the year 1772, on several parts of England; particularly the Mountains, and Lakes of Cumberland and Westmoreland* (1786).

—— *Observations, relative chiefly to Picturesque Beauty, made in the year 1776, on several parts of Great Britain; particularly the High-Lands of Scotland* (1789).

—— *Remarks on Forest Scenery, and other Woodland Views (relative chiefly to Picturesque Beauty) illustrated by the scenes of New-Forest in Hampshire* (1791).

—— *Three Essays: on Picturesque Beauty; on Picturesque Travel; and on Sketching Landscape: to which is added a poem, on Landscape Painting* (1792).

—— *Observations on the Western Parts of England, relative chiefly to Picturesque Beauty. To which are added, a few remarks on the picturesque beauties of the isle of Wight* (1798).

—— *Observations on the coasts of Hampshire, Sussex, and Kent, relative chiefly to picturesque beauty; made in the summer of the year 1774* (1804).

William Gilpin, *Observations on Several Parts of the Counties of Cambridge, Norfolk, Suffolk, and Essex. Also on Several Parts of North Wales; relative chiefly to Picturesque Beauty, in Two Tours, the former made in the year 1769. The latter in the year 1773* (1809).

George Mason, *An Essay on Design in Gardening* (1780).

Horace Walpole, *The History of Modern Taste in Gardening* (1780).

William Shenstone, *Essays on Men and Manners* (1802). (Posthumous.) 'Unconnected thoughts on Gardening.'

Uvedale Price, *An Essay on the Picturesque* (1794).

Richard Payne Knight, *The Landscape, a poem* (1794).

Humphrey Repton, *Observations on The Theory and Practice of Landscape Gardening* (1803).

William Combe, *Tour of Dr. Syntax in Search of the Picturesque* (1812).

Secondary sources

Kenneth Clark, *Landscape into Art* (Oxford, 1949).

Christopher Hussey, *The Picturesque* (London, 1927).

D. H. Lawrence, 'Introduction to these Paintings' (1929), *Phoenix* (London, 1936).

Elizabeth Wheeler Manwaring, *Italian Landscape in Eighteenth Century England* (Oxford, 1925).

William D. Templeman, *The Life and Work of William Gilpin* (University of Illinois Press, 1939).

Primary sources   Chapter 4: Drama and poetry

William Shakespeare, *The Complete Works*, ed. W. J. Craig (Oxford, 1905).

Molière, *Tartuffe, ou l'Imposteur* (1664), adapted by Colley Cibber, and Isaac Bickerstaffe (1768).

William Congreve, *The Way of the World* (1700).

Edward Moore, *The Gamester* (1753).

John Home, *Douglas* (1756).

George Colman (the elder), *Polly Honeycombe* (1760).

—— *The Clandestine Marriage* (1766).

Oliver Goldsmith, *She Stoops to Conquer* (1773).

Richard Brinsley Sheridan, *The Rivals* (1775), *The Critic* (1781), and *The School for Scandal* (1783).

Richard Cumberland, *The Wheel of Fortune* (1795).

George Colman (the younger), *The Heir at Law* (1797).

Mrs Elizabeth Inchbald, *Lovers' Vows*; from the German of Kotzebue (1798).

John Milton, *The Poetical Works*.
James Thomson, *The Seasons* (1726–30).
Alexander Pope, *Poetical Works*.
Dr Samuel Johnson, *London* (1738) and *The Vanity of Human Wishes* (1749).
Gilbert West, *Education*, a poem (1751).
William Cowper, *Poems* (1782, 1785).
George Crabbe, *The Village* (1783), *The Parish Register* (1807), *The Borough* (1810), *Tales* (1812).
William Wordsworth and S. T. Coleridge, *The Lyrical Ballads* (1798).
Henry Francis Cary, Translation of Dante, *The Inferno* (1805), *The Purgatorio* and *The Paradiso* (1812).
William Wordsworth, *Poems* (1807).
Sir Walter Scott, *The Lay of the Last Minstrel* (1805), *Marmion* (1808), *The Lady of the Lake* (1810).
Lord Byron, *The Giaour* (1813), *The Bride of Abydos* (1813), *The Corsair* (1814).

Secondary sources

F. W. Bateson, *English Comic Drama, 1700–1750* (Oxford, 1929).
René Huchon, *George Crabbe and His Times* (London, 1907).
A. Nicoll, *A History of Late Eighteenth Century Drama, 1750–1800* (revised edition, Cambridge, 1952).
J. Palmer, *The Comedy of Manners* (London, 1913).

PART II: THE TRADITION IN THE NOVEL

Primary sources   Chapter 5: The beginnings

John Bunyan, *The Pilgrim's Progress*, Part 1 (1678) and Part 2 (1684), *The Life and Death of Mr Badman* (1680).
Samuel Richardson, *Pamela* (1740), *Clarissa* (1748) and *Sir Charles Grandison* (1753–4).
Henry Fielding, *Joseph Andrews* (1742), *Jonathan Wild* (1743), *Tom Jones* (1749) and *Amelia* (1751).

Secondary sources

A. Block, *The English Novel, 1740–1850*. A catalogue, including Prose Romances, Short Stories, and translations of foreign Fiction (London, 1939).
Frank W. Bradbrook, 'Samuel Richardson', *The Pelican Guide to English Literature*, vol. 4 (London, 1957).
A. Dobson, *Samuel Richardson* (London, 1902).
B. W. Downs, *Samuel Richardson* (London, 1928).

F. Homes Duddon, *Henry Fielding, His Life, Works and Times* (Oxford, 1952).

A. D. McKillop, *Richardson, Printer and Novelist* (Chapel Hill, North Carolina, 1936).

—— *The Early Masters of English Fiction* (Lawrence, 1956).

Leslie Stephen, *Hours in a Library* (London, 1909), 'Richardson's Novels', vol. I; 'Fielding's Novels', vol. II.

Henri Talon, *John Bunyan, The Man and his Works* (London, 1951).

Ian Watt, *The Rise of the English Novel* (London, 1957).

Primary sources   Chapter 6: *The Feminist tradition*

Sarah Fielding, *David Simple* (1744).

Charlotte Lennox, *The Female Quixote* (1752).

George Ballard, *Memoirs of Several Ladies of Great Britain* (Oxford, 1752).

Frances Sheridan, *Memoirs of Miss Sidney Biddulph* (1761).

Frances Brooke, *Lady Julia Mandeville* (1763).

Fanny Burney, *Evelina* (1778), *Cecilia* (1782) and *Camilla* (1796).

Clara Reeve, *The Old English Baron* (1778), *The Progress of Romance* (1785).

Mme de Genlis, *Adelaide and Theodore* (1783), *Les Veillées du Château* (1784), *Alphonsine* (1806).

Charlotte Smith, *Emmeline, or the Orphan of the Castle* (1788), *Ethelinde, or the Recluse of the Lake* (1790), *The Old Manor House* (1793).

Mrs Elizabeth Inchbald, *A Simple Story* (1791).

Ann Radcliffe, *The Romance of the Forest* (1791), *The Mysteries of Udolpho* (1794), *The Italian* (1797).

Mrs Parsons, *The Castle of Wolfenbach* (1793), *The Mysterious Warning* (1796).

Mrs Jane West, *A Gossip's Story* (1796).

Regina Maria Roche, *The Children of the Abbey* (1798), *Clermont* (1798).

Eleanor Sleath, *The Orphan of the Rhine* (1798).

Maria Edgeworth, *Castle Rackrent* (1800), *Belinda* (1801), *Patronage* (1814).

Mme de Staël, *Corinne, ou l'Italie* (1807).

Hannah More, *Coelebs in Search of a Wife* (1809).

Jane Austen, *Sense and Sensibility* (1811), *Pride and Prejudice* (1813), *Mansfield Park* (1814), *Emma* (1816), *Northanger Abbey* and *Persuasion* (1818). *The Novels*, ed. R.W. Chapman (third edition, Oxford, 1933). *Minor Works*, ed. R.W. Chapman (Oxford, 1954). *Letters*, ed. R. W. Chapman (second edition, Oxford, 1952).

BIBLIOGRAPHY

Secondary sources

E. Birkhead, 'Sentiment and Sensibility in the Eighteenth-century Novel', *Essays and Studies of English Association*, vol. XI (1925).

Anne K. Elwood, *Memoirs of the Literary Ladies of England from the commencement of the last century*, 2 vols. (London, 1843).

Joyce Hemlow, *The History of Fanny Burney* (Oxford, 1958).

R. Brimley Johnson, *The Women Novelists* (London, 1918).

Alicia Lefanu, *Memoir of Mrs Sheridan* (London, 1824).

B. G. MacCarthy, *The Later Women Novelists, 1744–1818* (Oxford, 1947).

M. Reynolds, *The Learned Lady in England, 1650–1760* (Cambridge, U.S.A., 1920).

Virginia Woolf, *A Room of One's Own* (London, 1929).

Primary sources   Chapter 7: *Other influences*

Jonathan Swift, *Works* (1755, 1784, and 1814).

Mme de Sévigné, *Letters* (1726, translated 1758).

Dr Samuel Johnson, *Rasselas* (1759).

F. M. Arouet Voltaire, *Candide* (1759), *Essai sur les mœurs* (1759 and 1769).

Jean-Jacques Rousseau, *La Nouvelle Héloïse* (1761), *Émile* (1762).

Laurence Sterne, *Tristram Shandy* (1760–67), *A Sentimental Journey* (1768).

Horace Walpole, *The Castle of Otranto* (1765).

Oliver Goldsmith, *The Vicar of Wakefield* (1766).

Henry Mackenzie, *The Man of Feeling* (1771).

Johann Wolfgang von Goethe, *The Sorrows of Young Werther* (1774, 1787).

Choderlos de Laclos, *Les Liaisons dangereuses* (1782).

Hugh Blair, *Lectures on Rhetoric and Belles Lettres* (1783).

Arnaud Berquin, *L'Ami de l'Adolescence* (1785).

Tobias Smollett, *Collected Works* (1790, 1796, and 1797).

James Boswell, *Life of Johnson* (1791, 1793 and 1799).

Mary Wollstonecraft, *The Rights of Woman* (1792).

Sir Egerton Brydges, *Mary de Clifford* (1792), *Arthur Fitz-Albini* (1798), *Revision of Collins's 'Peerage of England'* (1812), *Autobiography* (1834).

William Godwin, *Caleb Williams* (1794), *St Leon* (1799).

Peter Teuthold, *The Necromancer, or the tale of the Black Forest* (1794).

Peter Will, *Horrid Mysteries* (1796).

Francis Lathom, *The Midnight Bell* (1798).

BIBLIOGRAPHY

Robert Southey, *Life of Nelson* (1813).
Eaton Stannard Barrett, *The Heroine* (1813).
Sir Walter Scott, *Waverley* (1814).

Secondary sources

D. J. Greene, 'Jane Austen and the Peerage', *P.M.L.A.* vol. LXVIII, no. 5 (December 1953), pp. 1017–31.
Sir Leslie Stephen and Sir Sidney Lee, *The Dictionary of National Biography* and *Supplements* (various editions).
Mary Katherine Woodworth, *The Literary Career of Sir Samuel Egerton Brydges* (Oxford, 1935).

INDEX

INDEX

INDEX